Civil War Recollections of James Lemuel Clark

Series

from
Republic of Texas Press

RECOLLECTIONS
OF JAMES LEMUEL CLARK

and the Great Hanging at
Gainesville, Texas in October 1862

by James Lemuel Clark

Edited and with an Introduction by

L.D. Clark

Republic of Texas Press

Library of Congress Cataloging-in-Publication Data

Clark, James Lemuel, 1843-1932.
  Civil War Recollections of James Lemuel Clark and the great
  hanging at Gainesville, Texas, in October 1862 / edited and with
  an introduction by L.D. Clark.
        p.   cm.
  Includes bibliographical references.
  ISBN 1-55622-505-9 (pbk.)
    1. Clark, James Lemuel, 1843-1932--Diaries.   2. Soldiers--Texas--
    Diaries.   3. Texas--History--Civil War, 1861-1865--Personal
  narratives.   4. United States--History--Civil War, 1861-1865--Personal
  narratives, Confederate.   5. Hanging--Texas--Gainesville--History--
  19th century.   6. Gainesville (Tex.)--History.   I. Clark, L.D.   II. Title.
  E605.C584   1996
  973.7'82--dc20   96-5757
                                                                       CIP

Copyright © 1997 by L.D. Clark

All Rights Reserved

Printed in the United States of America

ISBN 1-55622-505-9
10 9 8 7 6 5 4 3 2 1
9607

All inquiries for volume purchases of this book should be addressed
to Wordware Publishing, Inc., at 1506 Capital Avenue, Plano, Texas
75074. Telephone inquiries may be made by calling:
                          (214) 423-0090

Contents

Illustrations

[9]

Preface

THE author of these recollections spelled errati-
cally and employed almost no punctuation. I have
regularized the names of persons and places and have
punctuated sparingly. If the author sometimes wrote
a word in standard spelling and sometimes not, I
have adopted the standard spelling throughout the
text. If he employed a number of nonstandard spell-
ings of a word, I have adopted the spelling that appears most frequently. Other idiosyncrasies of the
writing are retained as I found them. My purpose has
been to preserve the flavor of the style as much as
possible without a sacrifice of clarity.

Special thanks are due to the Elma Dill Russell
Spencer Foundation for helping finance the publication of this volume. I wish also to express my grati-
tude to the following persons: Margaret P. Hays of
the Cooke County Heritage Society for assisting me
with research materials, Harwood Hinton and Bruce
Dinges of *Arizona and the West* for directing me to Civil
War literature and lending me books, Cordelia Waggoner James for lending me family papers, Michael
Clark for his photographic work, and Miles Ray Clark
for helping me gather old photographs.

L. D. CLARK

Editor's Introduction

DURING his last years my grandfather wrote down these memories and the most troubling thoughts of a lifetime. He died at the age of ninety when I was ten, just old enough to recognize in his death the passing of an age. Children tend to think of even their parents not as so many years older than they are but as belonging to another time altogether, though a time still within their reach. The eighty years between my grandfather's birth and mine was a span so vast as to place his youth, for me, in some mysterious lost epoch that I could only faintly touch. Just as the long ago seemed always to hover about him, so did the far away. As a boy he had come by ox wagon from Missouri to Texas, not to the tame Texas that I knew but to a wilderness where grass stood waist high in the glades, and straight virgin post oaks covered the hills in even stands free of underbrush. That was also the Texas in which the light of the moon might bring Indian raids, Comanche or Kiowa braves as ancient to me as any warriors out of biblical days. All in all, if I had thought then according to an order, I would have placed the beginning of my grandfather's time just after the creation of the world.

Yet in some ways James Lemuel Clark kept his hold on youth. Up to his last illness he rode his gentle old mare around the countryside with only a towsack spread under him for a saddle. He was always ready to enter wholly into any pretending that his grandsons thought up, as when a bunch of us lay in wait by a trail through the woods near his house, descending on him as he passed like so many robbers out of a forest, with bandanna masks and cap pistols. He put on such a convincing show of surprise and fear that I felt my true identity slipping away from me, leaving me a bandit for sure. In a fright I lowered the bandanna from my face, to break the spell, to let him know who I really was. I spoke my name, and I was not sorry that I had done it, either, though two of my cousins laughed at me. I recognize now that I glimpsed in the make-believe of that moment another that he had the power to bring to life, make-believe that I knew well from evenings in front of the fireplace at home: the make-believe of his storytelling, in which the ghosts of Indians and bushwhackers and charging cavalry could suddenly edge up around him in the shadows of the lamplight.

It was a fine thing to visit Grandpa, too, in the old house of rough gray lumber whose rooms had the look of having been constructed separately and shoved haphazardly together, leaving the two wings to stand askew with a corridor between the kitchen and front room open to the world at both ends—the dog run, we called it. A crooked sandstone chimney had been inserted between that front room and a bedroom, making another unlikely gap. A trumpet vine ran up the east wall of the house and clutched at the shingles of the roof. In the yard stood two knobby post oaks, and had been standing there long enduring since many years before the house shouldered its way in. Grandpa lived there alone, a widower since before I was born, alone yet all but surrounded by the farms of his sons. It was a rare day that passed without at least one visit from a descendant. Even if no one dropped by, he could see his children and their children out in the broad sweep he commanded from his front porch, as they moved around and across their fields and pastures. On that porch we would often find him reading from one of two books: a Bible with chipped and flimsy leather covers or a battered *Pilgrim's Progress*, whose most fascinating pages were the ones with engravings in which countless tiny lines brought people and landscape to life in a dark and flowing clarity.

Sometimes one of his grandsons would find him on the porch not reading but writing laboriously with a pencil stub on school tablet paper, tracing out from distant memory the greatest adventures and the greatest tragedy of his lifetime, all crowded into the years of the Civil War. Not thinking to leave room for revisions, he would begin an account and then after a few pages, dissatisfied, start all over again, expanding and adding details but also at times dropping significant points from a preceding version. He wrote a letter to Congress, too, which he never mailed, outlining the tragedy of the "Great Hanging." He might also have lying before him the little fragments of statements that he had collected from witnesses to the hangings. For a number of years off and on he worked on these papers, and then, not long before he died, he put them all away in a trunk. When he died the papers were passed on to my father and eventually to me. In order to produce the coherent account of the following pages, I have threaded the several fragments together.

James Lemuel's parents were Nathaniel Miles Clark (1818–62) and Mahuldah Lutisha Hicklin Clark (1820–83). They were married 7 July 1841, probably in Missouri. James Lemuel was the oldest of their large family. The Clarks migrated to Cooke County, Texas, from Missouri just before the Civil War. Like most of those who made the trek at that time, the Clark family had little sympathy with the principles that led to secession. At least one member of James Lemuel's mother's family, the Hicklins, was a large slaveholder in Missouri. A story still told by descendants has it that James Lemuel's parents found his treatment of slaves so cruel that they objected to slavery more than they otherwise might have. The Clark family already had a long tradition of antislavery feeling reaching back to their Quaker ancestors in seventeenth-century Virginia.

With the outbreak of the Civil War, James Lemuel, at eighteen, faced inevitable military service for a cause in which he did not believe. Short of escape to the North, the best alternative was to volunteer for the state militia. The militia had been organized to control hostile Indians, who had been freed to raid north Texas at will by the withdrawal of the United

States Army from Indian Territory. Cooke County, bordering on the Red River, was one of the more vulnerable areas. The principal difficulty with this alternative service was that the militia units were subject to absorption by the Confederate army. James Lemuel joined a militia company in the spring of 1861 and was with the forces sent by the state of Texas to occupy Indian Territory forts soon after their abandonment by Union troops. Volunteering at Fort Cobb to accompany General Albert Pike on his expedition to draw up treaties between the Confederacy and various Territory tribes, James Lemuel was involved in a number of interesting episodes before his company was finally ordered back to north Texas that fall and was soon thereafter mustered into the Confederate army. Nathaniel Clark stepped in, however, and hired a substitute for his son, making it possible for him to return home for the time being.

The next step his father took to put James Lemuel beyond the reach of the Confederates was one to which a great many Unionists resorted. The boy enlisted in a company formed by a recent arrival from Missouri for the purpose of going back and entering Confederate service in that state. In one of the curious twists of attitude common to that harrowing era, the company commander, a relative on the Hicklin side, in effect promised the boy the opportunity to desert when they reached the vicinity of his mother's family in southern Missouri.

This company left Gainesville in the spring of 1862 and soon arrived at a location from which James Lemuel could easily have sought out his relatives. For reasons never fully explored, he did not do so. It may well have been that his Hicklin kinfolk, being plantation people, would have looked askance on his desertion. One of that family, it seems, even joined William Quantrill's Confederate guerrilla band. James Lemuel's company was incorporated into the Confederate army while he was still a member of it, and he spent a great many months campaigning against the Union with General Joseph Shelby's cavalry division. Because he was usually one of the youngest soldiers in any unit, he was often assigned to carry dispatches or to hold horses when the unit dismounted to fight.[1] In one engagement his ankle was injured by a frightened horse. The accident left him with a slight limp for the rest of his life.

Strangely enough, at a time when all was strange, it was not the son's life that turned out to be at stake but the father's, back home in Cooke County. Nathaniel Miles Clark was one of the more than forty men loyal to the Union who were rounded up and executed by Confederate extremists in the Great Hanging of October 1862. As letters appearing later in this book show, the son did not receive specific notice of this disaster until the following January, and, for reasons barely treated in these recollections, a few more months went by before he could manage to quit his military company and return home.

Once there, he tried to fill his father's shoes as well as he could at the age of twenty. But again the

[1] It was cavalry practice for one soldier to hold four horses, his own and three others, when the unit dismounted to go into battle.

only way to remain in the vicinity was to sign up with one of the units kept on the frontier to protect the white population from hostile Indians. James Lemuel volunteered for this kind of service and was accepted in one of the companies. This arrangement served his purpose well enough until the spring of 1864, when the same fate as before overtook his present outfit: the necessity of battlefield duty in a Confederate army now growing desperate for men. Worse yet, since not only he but many of his fellow home guardsmen were known to have Union leanings, the suspicions that the rabid southerners in the area had long harbored against them finally came to a head, putting their lives in jeopardy. Deserting again, James Lemuel joined others of like sympathies to form a band of refugees, including some women and children, a band strong enough to discourage rebel interference and to undertake the long, dangerous journey through wild country to Union lines. Making a wide circle to avoid hostile Indians, the band at last arrived at Fort Gibson, Indian Territory, a post which the rebels had occupied but which was by then safely back in Union hands. At this place James Lemuel was not long in volunteering as a scout for the United States Army. By then it was early 1865, and the War of the Rebellion was nearing its end. He was assigned to a detachment about to head for Texas. Its purpose was doubtless to spy out ways to ease an eventual Union invasion. The detachment was much delayed, in part by Indian attacks as they crossed the Territory (most of the manuscript pages describing this journey to

Texas are lost), and when they finally reached the first settlements along Red River, they learned that the war was over.

James Lemuel did what a host of others must have done: he simply went home, not bothering with the formality of a discharge. The few efforts he made thereafter to secure one never came to any conclusion. More of this later on. We turn back now to the lynchings that claimed the life of James Lemuel's father and other Unionists, and to the developments leading up to them.[2]

In 1860, with a population of nearly four thousand, Cooke County had sixty-six slaveowners and by one estimate three to four hundred slaves, at least half of whom were in the hands of a few large planters along Red River.[3] These men exerted power and influence far out of proportion to their numbers. They knew well enough how to play up the sectionalism without which the slavocrats of the South would never have been able to raise a rebellion against the

[2] Thomas Barrett, *The Great Hanging at Gainesville* (Gainesville, Texas, 1885; reprint, Austin, 1961; herafter cited as Barrett, *Hanging*); George Washington Diamond, "George Washington Diamond's Account of the Great Hanging at Gainesville, 1862," ed. Sam Acheson and Julie Ann Hudson O'Connell, *Southwestern Historical Quarterly* 66:331–414 (hereafter cited as Diamond, "Account"); Claude Elliott, "Union Sentiment in Texas, 1861–1865," *Southwestern Historical Quarterly* 50:449–77; James Smallwood, "Disaffection in Confederate Texas: The Great Hanging at Gainesville," *Civil War History* 22:349–60; Floyd F. Ewing, Jr., "Unionist Sentiment on the Northwest Texas Frontier," *West Texas Historical Association Yearbook* 33:58–70; H. A. Trexler, "Episode in Border History," *Southwest Review* 16:236–50; Philip Rutherford, "The Great Gainesville Hanging," *Civil War Times Illustrated*, April 1978, 12–20.
[3] Michael Collins, *Cooke County, Texas: Where the South and the West Meet* (Gainesville, 1981), 10; Lillian Gunter Papers (typescript, North Texas State University Library, Denton), 233.

United States. When the issue of secession came to a head, the planters manipulated the selection of delegates from Cooke County to the state convention. Still, when the resolution calling for Texas to secede was submitted to a popular vote, Cooke and six nearby counties as a block voted overwhelmingly against it. A petition was circulated calling for organization of a new state to seek admission to the Union, a move that probably would have been carried out if those counties had not been cut off geographically from loyal territory.[4]

All the same, the Unionists of north Texas found that they could endure the usurpation of the rebels, biding their time in the conviction that the regime could not last for long. What precipitated resistance to insurgent power, there and elsewhere, was military conscription and its inevitable abuses. The legislation was passed in its first form in April 1862. That no American government had ever before resorted to compulsory military service was in itself enough to stir resentment, even among avid Confederates, let alone Union loyalists. What caused most of the trouble were the exemption provisions, which after a long, heated controversy in the Confederate congress were extended in October of that year to include those who had charge of twenty or more slaves. It did not matter to those outside the planter class that this measure was taken to ensure continued operation of the agri-

---

[4] Collins, *Cooke County, Texas*, 10–11. The vote against secession in Cooke County was 221 to 137. For background see Floyd F. Ewing, Jr., "Origins of Unionist Sentiment on the West Texas Frontier," *West Texas Historical Association Yearbook* 33:21–29.

culture vital to the South. To a great many it was simply a flagrant move by the powerful slavocrats to avoid risking their own skins in a war being waged chiefly for their benefit.[5]

From Cooke County a petition protesting this exemption, signed by thirty or more, including James Lemuel's father, was submitted to the Confederate congress sometime during the legislative debate over extension of the exemption. This challenge to their power must have put the local slaveholders on their guard, but they did not learn for a while the extent to which Unionist opposition was rapidly growing. The Union League had come into being, a secret society with a system of signs and passwords, in communication with the Union army and perhaps also with guerrilla groups in Kansas. League members took an oath to offer all possible resistance to the rebel government, to promote restoration of the Union, and to come to the aid of any compatriot in trouble with Confederate authorities. Specific measures for carrying out the resolutions of the league were to be determined by circumstances.[6]

The insurrectionists first got wind of the league in early September 1862. One of its members, Ephraim Childs, expansive after whiskey, took the wrong man into his confidence, revealing the existence of the league and also a scheme to seize Confederate arms

[5] Albert Burton Moore, *Conscription and Conflict in the Confederacy* (New York, 1924; reprint, 1963), 63–65, 70–71, 73–74, 143–44, 153. James Lemuel Clark (hereafter JLC) states the minimum number of slaves to claim exemption as ten, apparently in error, though he may have had in mind a regional exemption made earlier. See Moore, *Conscription*, 129.

[6] Barrett, *Hanging*, 3, 10; Diamond, "Account," 375–77.

stored in Cooke and Grayson counties, most of them in a depot in Sherman. The supposed friend, J. B. McCurley, went to the Confederate military. As soon as word reached General William Hudson, the commanding officer of the district, and Colonel James Bourland, who was in charge of the Frontier Regiment, mobilized to protect the region from Indian incursions, the two officers wasted no time launching an investigation, with Colonel Bourland taking the lead. A ruthless Confederate partisan and one of the largest slaveholders in the county, Bourland had much to fear from the Union men, and the massacre that followed was all the bloodier for Bourland's exercise of pure self-interest. He sent McCurley back to Childs to join the league as an informer. Then, not content with what his spy had found out, he called in a fellow officer, Colonel Newton Chance, to attempt a full penetration of the league's designs. Strange as it may seem that a Confederate officer, whose strong convictions were well known, could so easily beguile a Union plotter, Chance later testified that Dr. Henry Childs, Ephraim's brother and a prominent league member, had admitted him to the order, revealed most of its plans, and given him the names of a great many members, all within hours of their first meeting.[7] Childs must have been swept away by overconfidence, since the league thus far in its quick growth had met with nothing but success. One estimate put the membership at 1,700 in a five-county area, and Childs claimed

---

[7] Diamond, "Account," 353–55, 374–77; Collins, *Cooke County, Texas*, 11. See also Part 2, n. 7, below.

that he had sworn in 50 men in one recent eight-day period.[8]

The information that Chance carried back to Bourland on the day of his initiation, 26 September, was more than sufficient to impel a man like Bourland to take drastic action. All of the militia was assembled as quietly as possible, messages were sent to Confederate military installations requesting reinforcements, and martial law was imposed. On the night of 30 September small units were dispatched to lie in wait near the homes of known Union men, and at dawn the next morning a large number of them were taken into custody, marched to Gainesville, and thrown in prison. The arrests went on for several days, with perhaps as many as 150 men seized and jailed.[9]

For a day or two afterward fears ran high in Gainesville that the league might be able to muster a force powerful enough to attempt a rescue of their comrades. One or two bands did gather for that purpose, but they were so far outnumbered by the several companies of Confederate troops in the town that they recognized the futility of an attack.[10]

A mob at once gathered in Gainesville, the more rabid members of which were already calling for a

[8] Gunter Papers, 230; Diamond, "Account," 355.

[9] Barrett, *Hanging*, 7–8; Diamond, "Account," 361–62; C. N. Jones, *Early Days in Cooke County* (Gainesville, 1936; reprint, 1977), 64–65; A. Morton Smith, *The First 100 Years in Cooke County* (San Antonio, 1955; reprint, Gainesville, 1976), 34–35; Gunter Papers, 230. Many arrests were also made in Grayson and other neighboring counties, but a stronger stand by military and civil authorities in those counties in favor of law and order prevented wholesale killings like those in Cooke County.

[10] Barrett, *Hanging*, 9; Diamond, "Account," 363–64.

wholesale lynching. Around noon on that 1 October the rebel leaders, civilian and military, got up a "citizens' meeting." Colonel William C. Young took over as chairman. Young, a highly respected man, was at home on sick leave from his regimental command. He shared with Bourland the dubious distinction of being one of the few large slaveholders in the county. Young readied for the crowd an address designed to fan emotions already at combustion point, an appeal for action in the midst of which his "hope that wisdom and moderation may characterize our further proceedings" was but one faint note, even though it was a note that might have influenced the outcome of the tragedy for the better if events of the coming days had transpired differently.[11] When Young ended his speech by asking the crowd, "In the name of humanity what shall be done?" someone took the next step in what was clearly a manipulated proceeding, moving that Young as chairman appoint a five-man committee to select a twelve-man "jury" for a "citizens' court." Naturally the mob approved. In this manner Young, acting for the slaveholders and their dupes, kept a tight control over appointments to the "jury." A mock legality was thus trumped up for the mass murders that the mob might have carried out anyhow, but at least without the hypocritical sham imposed by Bourland, Young, and their cohorts. As we might expect, seven of the twelve chosen for the jury were slaveholders, who went so far as to insist at first on a simple majority rule in the decisions for execution. No doubt

[11] Diamond, "Account," 366–67.

most of the other five members were ready enough to do the bidding of the slaveholders, but they had found a way to avoid any risk to their scheme.[12]

The execution committee met and drew up a set of resolutions, the most crucial of which they proceeded to ignore. Each case was to be heard separately. In fact, some "group trials" were conducted. Each defendant was guaranteed defense by attorney and the right of cross-examination and of witnesses called on his behalf. In fact, nothing of the kind was ever put into practice. A few of the accused were said to have been offered counsel and defense witnesses but to have declined.[13] It is difficult to believe that the men would not lift a finger to save themselves even though they were aware of how little they could do to evade the vengeance of rebels.

And so the mockery of the "trials" began. The charges brought were invariably stated as "conspiracy and insurrection" or as "disloyalty and treason." The only one of these charges that was conceivable, in all this bloody farce, was conspiracy, seeing that the defendants had not yet gone as far as "insurrection" and could scarcely have been guilty of "disloyalty" or "treason" against a usurping government to which they had never offered or owed any allegiance.

The first man brought before the committee, on 2 October, was Henry Childs, and later that day his brother, Ephraim, was hustled in. On the basis of declarations by Chance, McCurley, and others, the Childs

[12] Ibid., 367–70; Collins, *Cooke County, Texas*, 13; Barrett, *Hanging*, 9.

[13] Diamond, "Account," 369, 385–86.

brothers were speedily judged guilty, given the death sentence, and hanged.[14] This established a pattern to be repeated with few variations and chilling regularity for more than two weeks.

To reconstruct what happened and what lay behind it in precise detail is not easy, for the two accounts on which we are largely dependent, that of Thomas Barrett and that of George Washington Diamond, are suspect. Each man in his own way seeks to characterize the incident as a regrettable but necessary action performed by wise and public-spirited men who had no alternative but to do as they did or see the whole region plunged into chaos and bloodshed. Diamond's account was drawn from the records kept by the impromptu court, which had appointed two clerks for that purpose. Diamond had been a newspaperman before the war and in 1862 held a commission in the Confederate army. When he went to Gainesville not long after the affair to visit a brother who had helped round up the Unionists, he was entrusted with the court records with the understanding that he would write a thoroughgoing vindication of the hangings.[15] Not until the mid-1870s did he undertake to fulfill his promise, and what he produced was left unfinished and unpublished at the time of his death. He arranged some of the testimony from papers in his possession, though we have no way of knowing

---

[14] Ibid., 373–85. While Diamond gives the date of the first two hangings as 4 October, another account states that the brothers were hanged on 2 October. John Wheeler, Diary (manuscript, Morton Museum, Gainesville, Texas).

[15] Diamond, "Account," 337–40.

whether he transcribed it verbatim. He introduced a background of sorts and a narrative of events interspersed with commentary, all of it written in a determination to give a noble cast to the outrage, even to the extent of arguing that the action must have been right, since it was undertaken by the "best men" in the county. When every other argument failed, Diamond could approve a death sentence because the accused, even though he did not belong to the league, was "an outspoken enemy of the South and, in every way, considered a dangerous and bad man in Society." To make matters worse, while no one can say whether he himself destroyed the records, at best he seems to have taken no care to preserve them, though he did see to the preservation of his own manuscript. It is much to the credit of his descendants that they permitted its publication during the Civil War Centennial.[16]

The other account we owe to the Reverend Thomas Barrett, who played an anomalous role in the affair. A reluctant member of the "jury" but nevertheless convinced that he had done the right thing, Barrett published in 1885 at his own expense a recapitulation of events that amounted to an impassioned plea for understanding. He was motivated, he declared, by his certain knowledge that only the arrest of the Unionists had prevented them from going

[16] Ibid., 337–38 n. 1, 369–72, 397. The records may possibly have survived, at least until the 1920s. A letter to Lillian Gunter in 1925 suggests that Adam Hornback, then living in Grayson County, Texas, may have had in his possession not only the records of the trial but also papers taken from the condemned men. Gunter Papers, 232.

on a rampage of indiscriminate slaughter—though no such evidence ever emerged in the testimony he himself heard—that is, as we have it through Diamond, who would hardly have failed to include information so advantageous to the prosecution. Further, Barrett was positive that if he had not brought at least some moderation to the trials the committee would have condemned far more men than it did. In this, at least, he appears to have been right, though it is a curious sort of morality that draws its conclusions in such a fashion. Barrett's third justification does not do him the credit he seems to have thought it did: that his own life might have been in danger if he had refused to participate in condemning others to death. He need not have worried. No staunch Confederate ran any risk of a rope around his neck, the whole affair having been carefully orchestrated from start to finish by the military command, chiefly by Colonel Bourland. What reflects most of all on Barrett's judgment is that he was too naïve, self-deluding, and self-important ever to realize the extent to which he was being used by the slavocrats, though he does speak once of the "jury" as being under compulsion from "the crowd of soldiers on duty pushed on by influential men." [17]

While the Diamond and Barrett accounts differ in a great many ways, they have one irritating feature in common: the florid and pompous language that the nineteenth century was so adept at wreathing around ugly deeds, a style that often arouses suspi-

[17] Barrett, *Hanging*, 8, 12–16.

[29]

cion even of reported facts and gives a hypocritical turn to all that the two men have to say. As James Lemuel Clark observed in reference to the style of another would-be champion of the Great Hanging, all such diatribe rings "like a seventy-five cent bell."[18]

Nevertheless, examination and comparison of the two accounts make all too clear how little the league members were guilty of at the time of their arrest in comparison with what their accusers maintained as the basis for their death sentences. According to Diamond's quotation of Chance, Childs had told him about the vows of Union loyalty, of resistance to the Confederacy, and of mutual protection. Whether resistance would ever come to armed uprising depended on the course of events. If the Union army invaded, league members were to join militia units to get hold of weapons and once in battle to go over to the Union side. They could hardly have been expected to do anything else, since their homeland had become enemy territory, and their only alternative, refusal to fight for the Confederacy, would probably have meant facing a firing squad. If an invasion was delayed, then the league would act when it had won over to its cause two-thirds of the north Texas men who were not away in Confederate service, a goal that the league fully expected to reach in the near future. Then, without bloodshed if possible, they would demand the stores of military supplies in the region—much of it no doubt United States property appropriated by the rebels a short time before—

[18] See p. 106 below.

and take control of the whole territory for the Union. If the Union could not come to their aid quickly and a Confederate counterattack proved too much for them, they would retreat to federal lines.[19]

But none of this had yet taken place, nor had any other act in open defiance of the Confederacy. The rebel leaders would have been justified, for their own protection, in breaking up the league by the arrest and imprisonment of key members. But Bourland and others desired the prompt extermination of as many Unionists as possible, knowing well the loyalty they might easily command among county residents. This destruction they could best accomplish by creating the impression of a grave and present danger, and the impending raid on the Sherman arms depot provided the opportunity. We have no way of knowing who started it, but the rumor was soon abroad that the Confederate forces broke up the league on the very night when it was gathering to attack the arsenal and precipitate a general uprising. This misconception persisted even though, as mentioned before, no evidence came forth to verify it—a misconception that shared a long life with another: that the executed men were not Union loyalists at all but a gang of largely itinerant cutthroats.

What in fact happened is easy enough to establish. As Henry Childs told both McCurley and Chance, such a raid had been set for an earlier date but had been postponed until the league could achieve the strength to ensure success. Barrett saw fit to de-

[19] Diamond, "Account," 335, 375–76.

clare that the raid had failed to materialize because of a flood "sent in great mercy" to "frustrate the wicked and abominable designs" of the league, oblivious that the Providence with the rebels under its tender care could have been circumvented by carrying out the raid a day or two later.[20] The night in question must have been 11 September, the only day of storm and flood reported in John Wheeler's diary. It was most likely a day or two before that when Ephraim Childs blurted out so much to McCurley, for he spoke of making the raid "damned soon." When McCurley called on Henry Childs about two weeks later, Childs stated that the league had decided to postpone the raid "for a while," and this in turn agrees with what Childs said to Colonel Chance on 26 September.[21] The only basis for mistaking 30 September as the night the league meant to attack, if any basis was necessary, must have been a confusion between the anticipated counterattack by the league following the first arrests and the arms-depot raid, or even, since the raid was known to have been scheduled for a night when a downpour came, the coincidence that rain fell in some parts of the county on the night of the arrests.[22]

Thus the slavocrats did not have even this show of reason to justify the slaughter of their opponents. Nevertheless, the committee during its first few days

[20] Ibid., 354, 375; Barrett, *Hanging*, 11–13.
[21] Diamond, "Account," 354, 375.
[22] Collins, *Cooke County, Texas*, 11; Diamond, "Account," 361–62; Jones, *Early Days*, 64; Gunter Papers, 236. Barrett (*Hanging*, 7–8) does not mention any rain on the night of the arrests in the places where he was.

of sitting went through the motions of "justice" with great facility, dispatching to the gallows five other men besides the Childs brothers. According to Barrett, he himself pointed out that the formalities were needless, since by a majority proceeding all the prisoners were sure to hang. The slaveholders were clearly pulling together. To make matters worse, as Barrett saw it, some members of the committee felt compelled to find every defendant guilty, purely out of fear of the mob, whatever the evidence.[23]

Barrett then claims to have taken the risk of persuading the committee to adopt a two-thirds rule, and thus to have succeeded in freeing a number of men and in having others turned over to military headquarters. The two-thirds rule saved every man tried, for the time being, from going to the gallows. Barrett does not give numbers, while Diamond says that only three men were sent for trial by the military—all three, by the way, were hanged. As for the leniency of the committee itself, it may have been that by now a few members had slaked their thirst for revenge. But the mob and those who controlled it were not so easily appeased. At least twice they attempted a general lynching but were prevented by the guards, at the same time that the committee, according to Barrett, was clearing and releasing one man after another.[24] This procedure continued, it seems, for about a week. How large the mob was by this time would be difficult to determine; one would expect it to have diminished

[23] Barrett, *Hanging*, 13.
[24] Ibid., 15.

a great deal over a period of ten days or so. Barrett, of course, has every reason to stress how great and demanding the mob was. Whether or not it had shrunk to manageable size would have made no difference. Anything the mob desired, beyond outright storming of the jail, was sanctioned by the military force under Bourland's control, a force that was itself in effect a part of the mob.

Just how far the Bourland faction could go, and make use of the mob to do so, is evident in the next slaughter that took place. As Barrett has it, the turmoil had settled down enough by Saturday, 11 October, after ten days of trial and only seven executions, for the committee to make summary decisions on all the prisoners. Some would go to the military, and the rest would go free, they decided, but it seemed advisable to adjourn for a week without making any of the dispositions public. By the following Saturday the jury could probably reconvene, announce its decisions, and end the whole matter. But word leaked out, most likely through some member of the committee, since its decisions had been made in secret, and it now became clear how little control even the committee had over proceedings. Two mob leaders came to the meeting room and gave the committee an ultimatum: surrender twenty of the prisoners to be hanged, or the mob would hang them all. The "jury" meekly submitted, Barrett with the rest, at which point the chief mob spokesman selected the men he wanted from the committee's list, not twenty but fourteen.

Why these particular men were picked, Barrett does not say, beyond suggesting that some of them were simply unlucky because they were considered "prominent" in their neighborhoods. Yet he adds, one page later, that these fourteen were not among those who had been voted eligible for release when the committee reconvened but were those to be remanded to "headquarters of the military authority." In short, someone on the jury was cooperating hand in glove with the mob leaders; otherwise the identities of these fourteen and the judgment passed on them would not have been known to the mob. Someone wanted them dead and did not wish to take a chance on what might happen if they passed beyond the reach of the mob and its military support in Gainesville. As the mob spokesman left with the list, he said, according to Barrett, "I reckon that will satisfy them." Whether "them" might have been members of the mob or the Bourland faction is not ascertainable, but the distinction is hardly of consequence.[25]

During the two following days, 12 and 13 October, the fourteen men were hanged. Bourland provided a military escort for the mob to conduct its victims to the tree that served for all the hangings, a large elm on the banks of Pecan Creek, at the east edge of town.[26] Nathaniel Miles Clark was among those who died in this lynching, just as his tombstone reads: "Murdered by a mob, October 13, 1862."[27] As Barrett sat on the courthouse square in Gainesville watching the death processions pass, he could still ask himself

[25] Ibid., 16.
[26] Ibid., 8, 33.
[27] This gravestone, erected in 1878, mistakenly gives 1816 as Nathaniel Miles's birthdate.

—or so he wrote—whether it was possible that the military had known all along about the mob's plans. He pronounced the link between the mob and the military a "mystery" to him, even in the 1880s, when he was writing—which could only be self-deception, as a naïveté so blank could hardly be attributed even to him. But if Barrett found a conclusion too difficult to draw in this case, Diamond did not. He did not hesitate to call this butchery a "group trial," pretending that "testimony" like that against all the others had been produced and rounding off his description with the assurance that all the men—he named only twelve—"made full confession of their guilt at the gallows."[28]

The carnage might have stopped with these fourteen had it not been that on October 16 two men were killed from ambush in the Red River bottoms, one of them Colonel William Young.[29] No one could be certain who did the killing, whether it was fugitive members of the league, perhaps led by a Captain Garrison, an organizer from the North who had fled when the arrests began, or some of the renegade bands who had hideouts in the river brakes during the war years.[30] If the remnants of the league were responsible, they could not have done worse by their imprisoned compatriots. First of all, Colonel Young may have been about to intervene on behalf of the prisoners—James Lemuel Clark believed that Young was on his way to Gainesville for that purpose when he

[28] Barrett, *Hanging*, 17–18; Diamond, "Account," 397.
[29] Barrett, *Hanging*, 18–19.
[30] Diamond, "Account," 364–65.

[36]

was shot.[31] As we saw earlier, he was the only slave-holder on record for "wisdom and moderation," little as he had done to that end up to the time of his death. Like a few other cooler heads, he may have been near to having enough of the whole brutal business, and he had great influence. The course of events set in motion by his murder brought still more bloodletting. The blame fell on the league, of course, and the men still in custody were now treated as accessories to murder along with their other supposed crimes. Again, that Thursday of the shootings and the next day, talk of lynching ran wild. That the mob did not carry out its threats, when it could have done so far more easily than it had the previous weekend, leads again to the conclusion that the chief instigators were firmly in control of the situation. All they had to do was wait for the reassembling of the "jury" on Saturday, 18 October, for it was now apparent that a shadow of legality could be restored to the executions.

That is what happened, though the pretense of "justice" was by now thin indeed. The committee reversed all its decisions of the Saturday before and, as Barrett puts it, "placed the prisoners on trial the same as though they had not been tried."[32] He contends that he saved many lives that day, and he may well have done so. He seems to have recognized that his recommendations might now be heeded, and so he urged them strongly. Nineteen more men, by Barrett's count, were condemned that day, and "fifty or

[31] See p. 100 below.
[32] Barrett, *Hanging*, 20.

sixty" were freed.[33] The last victims were executed on Sunday, 19 October, bringing the reign of terror to an end. In three weeks, by Barrett's count, forty men had been hanged, two gunned down while attempting to escape, and some others turned over to the military. At least three of the last were convicted and executed, as pointed out, by court-martial. Two or three other men were later killed because of involvement of some sort with the league. The exact number of those who died in the whole affair is probably not ascertainable, for, as Barrett reports, several men may have been hanged or shot right after arrest, before they ever came to the notice of the committee.[34]

The scars this massacre left on the community and on every person it touched were a long time fading. The following pages speak eloquently of the later effects on the son of one of those who were killed. As previously stated, on learning of his father's murder, James Lemuel Clark went home as soon as he could to assist his mother and younger brothers and sisters— the youngest child was less than three years old. The military outfit he joined in order to remain in the region was, out of sheer necessity, Bourland's Frontier Regiment. One of the many ironies of the time was that this avid Confederate's command, as time went on, came to be made up more and more of Unionists. Thus he, along with Barrett and the other "jurors," had good cause to fear what these men might do when they were organized and armed.[35] The experi-

[33] Ibid., 21.
[34] Ibid., 19.
[35] Ibid., 22.

ences of James Lemuel Clark for the rest of the war are well presented in his own pages. In reference to the Great Hanging, his last comments, in the extant fragments, mention only a few years' difficulty after the war in establishing some kind of viable truce with the defeated rebels.[36] His first, and childless, marriage is known to have failed in part because of strong southern feeling in his wife's family. The Clarks for a time considered following the example of other families who had lost a member in the hanging—some of the perpetrators too, for that matter—and moving on to new territory.[37] Close friends who had migrated to Kansas urged the Clarks to join them, writing that Texas was fit only for "rebels and Indians." But James Lemuel went to look and came away of the opinion that Kansas was not for him. The parts of Arkansas that he had seen while serving under General Shelby came under consideration for a while as a new home. But when all was said and done, nothing suited James Lemuel like the Cross Timbers of Texas, and so he lived out his life there.[38]

Probably he would never have set down any account of his Civil War years had it not been for one especially infuriating revival of the Great Hanging in public discussion and his efforts in his old age to secure a pension.[39] No record was ever found of his

[36] See p. 92 below.

[37] W. R. Strong, *His Memoirs*, ed. Pete A. Y. Gunter and Robert A. Calvert (Denton, Texas), 46.

[38] Unpublished letter, Delia Kilborn to Cordelia Clark (JLC's sister), 1 November 186?; unpublished letter, JLC to his family in Texas, from Benton County, Arkansas, 30 November 1870.

[39] See p. 93 below.

brief enlistment in the United States Army, a confusion made worse, no doubt, by his failure to make sufficient effort to obtain a discharge until after many years had passed. And, since he was at least a double deserter from Confederate service, he found it impossible to make a good case for a pension from the state of Texas, such as was eventually awarded to most Confederate veterans. No pension from any source ever came through, and all that is left of his efforts is the record of his service found in these pages.

The murderers of the Union men were never brought to justice. The halfhearted efforts made by United States authorities after the defeat of the insurrectionists came to nothing. The guilty men no doubt profited from the general amnesty. Barrett was convinced that some of them were able to buy off members of a grand jury, though nothing beyond his statement is known of this. Barrett found himself in a position that was perhaps inevitable for one who so vehemently asserted his innocence, according to his own lights, by arguments that might be offered from either side, but in fact both sides considered him guilty. He had to go into hiding and lead a fugitive existence for some time after the war, when accusations, as he thought, were coming at him from all directions. He did eventually appear, voluntarily, before a grand jury and was quickly dismissed free of any charges.[40] And truly he did come in for more blame—or at least a different sort of blame—than his role warranted. And probably the more he protested,

[40] Barrett, *Hanging*, 22, 31, 33.

the more the blame was loaded on him. I remember a family tradition, told to me after James Lemuel's death, that Nathaniel Miles Clark was about to be released when Barrett declared that Clark was one of the prime conspirators and thereby sealed his fate. Yet this does not sound at all like Barrett. The story was more than likely a distortion of what happened when the execution committee decided in secret to release all the prisoners and then had to surrender the fourteen to the mob, Nathaniel Miles among them. Thus perhaps one of the two mob leaders became identified with Barrett.

As far as I can remember, this story was attributed to Nathaniel's widow, not to James Lemuel. He had his own convictions about who the villains were. He did not even place the blame for his father's death on Colonel Bourland, who he felt was deceived by others not named in his account.[41] The man he held most responsible was, I suspect, one of the mob leaders who ticked off the fourteen names for lynching. This much I remember clearly: James Lemuel swore vengeance on that man, and only him, as far as I know. He waited for the right moment, some years after the war. Then he went with a gun to the man's farm, surprising him at work in his barn. To shoot this man down in cold blood had seemed to James Lemuel no more than he deserved for what he had done. The man fell to his knees and begged for his life. James Lemuel found that at the moment of crisis he simply could not shoot any man under such condi-

[41] See p. 100 below.

tions. So he spared his life, and he never regretted his decision.

Not much is known about how many of the murderers had conscience enough to suffer from regrets. Barrett's protestations of right action under appalling circumstances are haunted by remorse. A man who interviewed him near the end of his life found his attempts at justification interrupted by tears.[42] And if James Lemuel felt that justice had been thwarted when he showed mercy to the man he had tracked down, he may finally have felt some consolation besides contempt for his cowardice. The man went crazy before he died, perhaps out of guilt, perhaps, as some said, out of the fears of vengeance that came to dominate his life.

Events like the Great Hanging become legendary almost from the time they are taking place, with all the fascination and distortion that legend brings. Some months later, on 20 February 1864, *Frank Leslie's Illustrated Newspaper* of New York carried a large engraving of several men hanging from the limbs of trees and an account dealing in part with the Gainesville hangings, under the heading "Rebel Outrages in Texas." The chief source of this story was Frank Sumner, a member of the league who fled from Sherman just ahead of the rebel crackdown. This article is accurate enough in outline, but it puts the number who perished at over one hundred and adds that James Young, in revenge for his father's murder,

[42] Unpublished Papers of G. H. Ragsdale, dated 12 September 1891 and 2 April 1892 (Cooke County Heritage Society Archives, Gainesville, Texas).

"caused 20 men to be hung the next day before breakfast." As a captain commanding a company of frontier rangers, Young court-martialed and hanged three men sent to him by the jury. Convinced that a man by the name of Dan Welch had killed their father, Young and his brother John hunted down Welch and brought him back for hanging at the spot where Colonel Young fell. Then, when Junius Foster, Unionist editor of the *Sherman Patriot,* refused to retract a public statement approving the assassination of the father, James Young shot him down.[43]

Other distortions of the Great Hanging crept in through determination to put either the victims or the perpetrators in the worst light possible, depending on who was describing the incident. At least two accounts place all the hangings after the furor caused by the shooting of Colonel Young, apparently for the purpose of making the motives of the mob leaders more understandable.[44] One of the accounts, maintaining that the victims were simply criminals who received their just deserts, speaks of a belief that these men had plotted to seize all the property they could and flee to Arizona—after slaughtering all the women and children, naturally. The source of this error was clearly the report that the league used "Arizona" as one of its passwords.[45] Many years later a son of one of the hanged men identified the leader of the Con-

[43] Diamond, "Account," 344 n. 7, 359 n. 22, 402–404; Jones, *Early Days,* 65–66; Gunter Papers, 224, 229.

[44] Gunter Papers, 222; Jones, *Early Days,* 65.

[45] Gunter Papers, 222; Barrett, *Hanging,* 10; Diamond, "Account," 391.

federate faction as Hugh Boland, chief of a band of "mixed breeds and lawless whites" who terrorized the county from their Red River hideout, and his partner as "a renegade from Mississippi, named Nut Chance." This account goes on to report a battle in which the Unionists first captured the "Boland" gang but were then defeated by units of the Confederate army, tried, and hanged, their number being about sixty. Possibly the writer here has tangled elements from two or more incidents.[46]

The scene of the hangings also held an attraction for many. The "old historic tree, that old elm" soon became an object of horrified curiosity. By 1884 some-one—reportedly a man by the name of Tom Williams—had cut down the tree and hauled the trunk to some unidentified place, where Barrett thought of it as lying dead like the men hanged from its limbs.[47] Fortunately his account of the tragedy did not disappear like the tree, though a long time went by before either his or Diamond's text emerged for public distribution. Other contemporary records of what occurred may still exist and may yet come to light. Descendants of those who took part on either side of the incident have always been understandably reluctant to allow any writing they possess on the subject to be printed. The following recollections were held back for years out of respect for objections by members even of the third generation from Nathaniel Miles

[46] Letter from John Mancil Crisp to George M. Crisp, 20 October 1921 (archives of the Morton Museum, Gainesville, Texas).
[47] Barrett, *Hanging*, 17, 33; Gunter Papers, 227.

Clark, now all passed on, though copies of this text made for family members some twenty years ago have found their way into other hands. That version was incomplete and hurriedly edited. The text of this book is more authoritative.

Civil War Recollections of James Lemuel Clark

I.

My father, Nathaniel Miles Clark, came to Texas in the year 1857, I think in October. We started from Cedar Co. Mo., stoped in Carroll Co. Ark. a fiew years, then came on to Texas. I was borned in what was called Dade Co., now Cedar, the year 1843. My father was borned and raised in Christian Co. Kentucky. When we came to Cooke County I was about 14 years old. We settled on the land we now own, a homestead of 160 acres 7 miles South East of Gainesville.[1]

---

[1] The following account was put together from several fragments written between 1916 and 1926. James Lemuel Clark died in 1932. Nathaniel Miles Clark was born in 1818 and died, as described in the Editor's Introduction, in the Great Hanging at Gainesville in 1862. In one of the two accounts combined here, dated 9 March 1926, JLC adds the following: "[We] had the land surveyed by George Y. Bird, the County Surveyor, in the year 1859. All went well until 1860, when a man by the name of E. C. Palmer come in an located the Hiram Walker Survey an surveyed Father in. After some trouble Walker agreed to murge Fathers premtion in an let it be patented to him. Walker agreed to make Father a deed to 160 acres out of his survey, which he did. Then in 1861 this man Palmer got in to trouble in Gainesville an tha got him in jail over the war. Tha found some papers that he had in his posesion shoing him to be for the North. His home was in Illinois. So he wrote Hiram Walker to come at once an git him out of jail. Walker lived in Limestone Co. Texas. Walker came to Gainesville to help him out. Palmer had been in Gainesville some time an boarded at W. W. Foremans Hotel an owed Foreman a bout $60 an some other debts. An Walker wanted Father to take the block of land

My father hued the logs to build the first jail that was built in this country. The jail was built near wher the Santa Fe Depo now is. An old man Gossett an Tom his boy hauld the logs as Father hued them. Of corse I helped all I could.[2]

We had no roads in the county then. Had to take our corse wher we wanted to go an travle threw the woods. That was the year 1859. In 1860 the country settled up, an [we] begun to open up roads and build school houses in the country. My father was made overseer to open up the Pilot Point Road, an William Howeth was made overseer on what was called the Preston Road, now the Callisburg Road. Tha were the first roads worked in the county. I think the oald Ranger Trace run threw the county E an West. The Mexicans made it from oald Fort Towson to Red River Station. The Rangers travled it all so in the year 48, an up to 50.[3] There camps were very plane to be seen

---

joining the 160 acres he had deeded him an pay Foreman the hotel bill an other debts, which Father did. An Walker made him a deed to the block of land, made the deed by giving meats and bounds, by other surveys suposed to be 240 acres in all, with 160 deducted out. It must be remem-berd that J. M. Lindsay was Walkers attorney. In fact, as the record shows, I was present an herd the agreement with Walker an Lindsay. Lindsay was to make my mother a warantee deed to all the land acorden to the face of the bonds, an Lindsay was to have the remainder at 50 cents an acre, after all bonds were sadisfide, which he did, as the record shows. This is a plot of the land that Walker deeded to the ares of N. M. Clark an Mary E. Clark." JLC goes on here to give the measurements of the land in question, perhaps because of some continuing dispute about ownership, and then breaks off after these measurements and begins another account.

    [2]The commissioners' court authorized construction of this jail on 19 May 1857, later awarding the contract to F. N. Hackney. Smith, *First 100 Years*, 25; Jones, *Early Days*, 17.

    [3]For a differing identification of the Ranger Trace, or Trail, see Strong, *His Memoirs*, 16–18. JLC's reference to Mexican use of a route through Cooke County may stem from the existence of an early Spanish

when we came to Cooke County. Tha were a fortafide camp at what now is called the Limestone Spring, a bout 2 hunderd yards South of the Six Mile school house. Tha had dug a rifle pit or 2. Tha were very well fortafide. I doant no how long tha were thare, but from the looks of every thing tha faught the Indians often. The Indians knew wher the spring was, for tha allwayes stade a round when tha would slip in the settlements in dry hot weather.

The first school house that was built in the country was the Dye. My father helped to build partly on it. It was named for a man by the name of Jake Dye, a Christian preacher. He was a leader in the settlement when we came to the country, an a good man. The first school that was taught in our settlement was taught by old Sammy Crisp. We had no free schools then, subscription schools. He taught for one dollar a month an very fiew to teach. That was the first school I ever went to. We was a fraid to go in light night of the moon, as the Indians was bad light moons. Tha was no roads to the schoolhouse, an all that sent would hich a yoke of oxon to a log an drag the grass down for a road. That was in 1858. The next school

---

road that ran along the south bank of the Red River. Frontier "rangers" under various types of organization patrolled the Red River frontier from the time of Texas independence in 1836, and for a time the Texas Rangers maintained an outpost at Preston. Fort Towson, in southeastern Oklahoma, was established in 1824 and was active off and on until it was abandoned in 1859. The Confederate army made use of it during the Civil War. Odie B. Faulk et al., eds., *Early Military Forts and Posts in Oklahoma* (Oklahoma City, 1978), 9–25. Red River Station, in Montague County, just west of Cooke County, became a crossing of importance in 1857. During the period of the Confederacy it was a fortified outpost of the Frontier Regiment, whose task was to guard against Indian depredations, and remained an active town through the cattle-driving days, until 1876.

was taught by Mrs. Jordan, an the next by my Aunt Cynthia Clark. The next by a man by the name of Graham. This was before the war, up to 1860. I never went to school more than 5 or 6 months in all my life all put to geather, on a count of the Indians. The last school was taught by Fathers brother, Jim Clark, in 59.

[My father] was a Democrat of the oald school. He voted for Stephen A. Douglas in the year 1860, tho he oposed cesesion an thaught the South ought to stay in the Union and fight for there rites.[4]

My father sent me out when [I] was only a boy in the state service. I will give a brief history of my inlistment. A bout the first of April 1861, I was sworn in by W. C. Twitty in Gainesville, Texas, in W. C. Twittys Co, Young's Regiment.[5] I came home [then], to report back in May. Which I did. A bout the first of May 1861, I left Gainesville under Twitty as Capton, Alex-

---

[4] Douglas was nominated the Democratic presidential candidate by the national convention at Charleston. He favored "popular sovereignty," by which states and territories would decide for themselves on the slavery issue, but he was at the same time a fervent supporter of the Union. Southern Democrats broke away from the national party because of Douglas's nomination.

[5] JLC wrote "Boaling [Bourland] regiment," but Bourland was commander of the military unit to which JLC belonged later. Bourland was, however, an officer in Young's regiment at this time. Gunter Papers, 97. See n. 38 below. Colonel William C. Young, a leader in Texas affairs from the 1830s and a planter in the Red River bottom country after 1858, was asked by Governor Edward Clark soon after secession to raise a cavalry regiment of north Texas volunteers for protection of the frontier against Indian raids and for other military necessities. Clement A. Evans, ed., *Confederate Military History* (Atlanta, 1899), vol. 11, *Texas*, 47, 56; Diamond, "Account," 366 n. 33. Captain William C. Twitty was an early settler in Cooke County. His company was the first to be formed in the Young regiment. The name James Lemuel appears on the roster as though Lemuel were a surname. There may be some confusion between this and the two Clark names, J. W. and J. D., also found in the roster. Smith, *First 100 Years*, 30–31; Diamond, "Account," 352 n. 16.

ander Boutwell as First Lieutenant, Sam Brough as 2 Lieutenant, Samuel H. Miller as 3 Lieutenant. We went to Montague Town and stade there a fiew dayes, an had our horses an equipment valued. We went from thare to Fort Arbuckle. When we got thare we found the oald Regulars gone. Tha had been orderd a way a fiew dayes before we got thare. We found every thing in very nice shape, a little must up. Good houses to stay in. Tha were I gess 25 hunderd bushels of oats in a long shed, but tha had beat glass fine an throde in them, an we was a fraid to feed them to our horses. Tha fixed every thing so we got no good out of eney thing tha left.[6]

We stade at Arbuckle sevrel dayes. I doant remember how long. But it wasnt long, because the Indians were all turned loose when the oald solgers left Fort Cobb an Arbuckle. In June or July 1861, we were orderd to oald Fort Cobb on the extreme frontier.[7] When we got thare every thing was in a bad fix. The oald solgers was orderd a way a fiew dayes before

[6] Fort Arbuckle was evacuated by federal troops on 4 May 1861 and occupied by Texas militia the following day. If Smith's date for the organization of Twitty's company is correct, then JLC's remembered date is not quite exact. The Twitty company need not have been the first to arrive. E. B. Long and Barbara Long, *The Civil War Day by Day: An Almanac, 1861–65* (New York, 1971, hereafter cited as Long and Long, *Civil War*); Smith, *First 100 Years*, 31; Gunter Papers, 97, 235.

[7] Union troops had carried out an orderly withdrawal from all this region of Indian Territory. In April forces from some outlying areas were gathered at Fort Washita. Under the command of Lieutenant Colonel W. H. Emory, they abandoned this fort on 30 April, retreating north, just one day before a unit of Texas militia arrived to take possession. By 9 May federal troops from Fort Cobb and Fort Arbuckle had joined Emory's column, which made its way to Fort Leavenworth, Kansas. The Texas militia had taken over Fort Cobb on 14 May. Long and Long, *Civil War*, 60, 67–70, 72; Lary C. Rampp and Donald L. Rampp, *The Civil War in the Indian Territory* (Austin, 1975), 3–5.

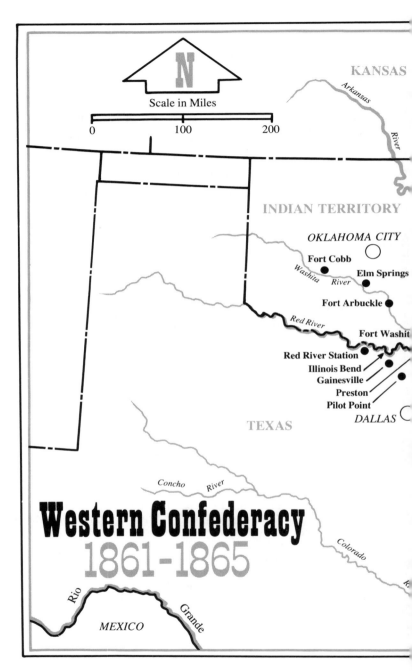

N

Scale in Miles

0   100   200

KANSAS

Arkansas

River

INDIAN TERRITORY

OKLAHOMA CITY ◯

Fort Cobb ●

Washita   *River*

Elm Springs ●

Fort Arbuckle ●

Red River

Fort Washit

Red River Station ●

Illinois Bend
Gainesville
Preston
Pilot Point

DALLAS ◯

TEXAS

Concho   *River*

Western Confederacy
1861-1865

Colorado

Rio

Grande

MEXICO

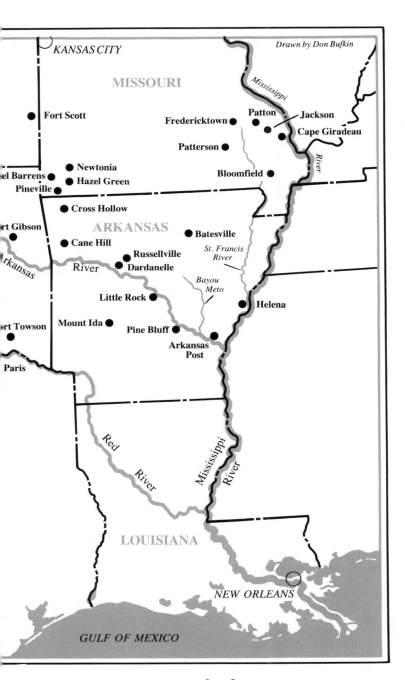

KANSAS CITY

MISSOURI

Fort Scott

Fredericktown ●

Patton

Jackson

Cape Giradeau

Patterson ●

Newtonia ●
el Barrens ●

Hazel Green ●

Bloomfield ●

Pineville ●

Cross Hollow ●

rt Gibson ●

ARKANSAS

Batesville ●

Cane Hill ●

Russellville ●
Dardanelle ●

St. Francis
River

rkansas

River

Bayou
Meto

Little Rock ●

Helena ●

Mount Ida ●

rt Towson ●

Pine Bluff ●

Arkansas
Post

Paris

Red

River

Mississippi

River

LOUISIANA

Mississippi

River

NEW ORLEANS

GULF OF MEXICO

Drawn by Don Bufkin

[55]

we got thare. Tha had burned the comasery, or tride to. Tha had used glass all so in all tha could not burn. Every thing looked screaky to me, the country full of Comanche Indians all on the war path. When the oald solgers were orderd a way, all the Indians left the reserve an painted up for a raid on the frontier of Texas. But we sorter gave them a little scare an tha luld up some. A fiew dayes after we got to Fort Cobb, Diamond's Company came.[8] We had a little spat or two with the Comanches. Tha were not as bad as the Kiowas. Oald Lone Wolf was a mean oald rat. He was head chief next to oald Kickapoo Joe.[9] Of corse we held the fort. I gess all told tha were a bout a hunderd an 75 or so men in boath companies. But the Indians was a fraid to come a bout.

A long in August 61, General Albert Pike was sent to Fort Cobb by the Confederacy to make a treaty with the Indians. He was sent from Little Rock, Arkansas.[10] Doant no how he came. He came in one night. We was all in line an on role call when he first showed up earley one morning. He walked up an

[8] According to one source, J. J. Diamond was commander of this company. Another has it that James J. Diamond was lieutenant colonel of the Young regiment from the time of its founding. The Diamond of this company was probably another of the six brothers of this family, possibly John R. Diamond. Smith, *First 100 Years*, 31; Diamond, "Account," 337 n. 1, 352 n. 15.

[9] No identification of Kickapoo Joe has been found. Lone Wolf was an important Kiowa leader, though little is known about him before 1867, when he is named by some as a signer of the Medicine Lodge Creek Treaty. He was one of the last challengers to white occupation of his homeland, taking part in several fierce raids before submitting in 1875.

[10] A Little Rock lawyer prominent in Arkansas affairs, Albert Pike had learned something about how to deal with Indians by traveling through their country several years earlier and by serving as legal repre-

looked us over a fiew minutes, an talked to our Capton Twitty some. Capton Twitty toald us who he was, an said he Pike wanted 2 men to voluntear to go with him to make a treaty with the Indians. An if eney of us wanted to go, step 2 paces in front of the line. So me an a man by the name of John McCrory steped out. A bout that time I saw 2 or 3 of my neighbor boys go up an speak to the capton. An he spoke to me an said I had beter step back in line. The boys was not willing for me to go. An I rather insisted. I wanted to go. Finaly Pike said, "I had as soon have that boy as eney man you have got."

So Twitty toald me, "All rite then."

So General Pike toald me an McCrory to git our breakfast an feed our horses an report at head quarters. We called Twittys home head quarters. So as quick as we got ready we went an found Pike at head quarters. Mrs Twitty had baked a hole lot of bread for us to take a long.[11] Pike said he did not no how long we would be gone.

---

sentative for some tribes. In May 1861 he received an appointment from Jefferson Davis, president of the Confederacy, as a special commissioner to the Territory tribes. Setting out at once on his mission, he succeeded in persuading most of the Civilized Tribes to become allies of the Confederacy, though many of the Cherokees submitted unwillingly, and the Creeks remained openly split. Pike reached the Wichita agency, near Fort Cobb, on 6 August 1861, hoping to bring about Confederate treaties with the roving Comanches and Kiowas as well as the agency Indians. Albert Pike, *Report of Albert Pike, Commissioner of the Confederate States to the Indian Nations West of Arkansas* (Richmond, Va., 1861; reprint, Washington, D.C., 1968), 7–20; *Confederate Military History*, vol. 10, *Arkansas*, 126.

[11] Elizabeth Montague Twitty was the daughter of Daniel Montague, a pioneer citizen of Texas from the beginning of the Republic. Montague County, Texas, bears his name. He was later "president of the court" in the Great Hanging episode. Diamond, "Account," 352 n. 16, 359 n. 22, 370.

We got ready an made the start.

We went West the first day. I doant no how far we travled that day, as Pike used his spie glass a good deale. We stoped that night an het our supper, let our horses graze an rest. We killed a bufalo calf an dun fine, shot a cogar a little after dark that wanted to stay with us an git our fresh meat. That nite Pike kept one man on gard at a time, while the others slept. We would move our horses a round the camp on fresh grass during the nite.

The second day we travled South West. Doant no how far we went. Pike would clime them high peakes an use his spie glasses often, an look in every direction for Indians. He had 2 spie glasses, one big one he said would draw an object 30 or 40 miles. The 2 day we stoped before nite on a count of water, as it was scarce. We found some sign of Indians that evning.

The 3 day we still travled more West. A long in the day a bout 2 oclock, Pike clum a high peak an we stade at the foot of the hill with the horses. We seen Pike take his little glass an look for some time. He then taken his big glass an looked for some time. We seen he had seen something. He holowed to us an said for two of us to come up thare at a time an look threw the glass. Which we did. Me an John McCrory went an looked. It looked like the hole western country was full of Indians. An the other two went an looked—tha were only fore of us besides Pike. But I have forgoten there names. Tha belonged to Diamonds Co.

Pike said the Indians were a bout 5 miles off. But

you could see the paint on there faces plane. Tha did not look good by a hole lot.

We was not long starting after them. Before we made the start Pike toald us if eney of us was the least bit scart to say so an drop out at once. For it would not do to wilt the least bit, for we had to ride to them. We were all ready to make the run on them, to folow Pike.

The Indians were travling NE when we spide them out, an we were North of them. So Pike said he would go South East an cut in the near way. We rode off in a trot an run to git a head of them. An sure anuff we struck the lead bunch [after] a bout 2 miles travle. When we got in sight of the lead ones, Pike made a little hault an toald us what we mite expect. How tha would do when tha saw us. He said tha would cut all maner of shines. Tha would draw arows like tha were going to shoot, an try to ride over us, but for us to folow him an pay no atension to them. An for us not to gase a round. An if tha got in the way to ride over them. An if tha tride to cut us off, for us not to make no passes at them til he toald us to shoot. An to shoot to hurt.

An sure anuff tha did as he said. Tha were a bout 2 hunderd in the bunch. Tha was badly scart when we run in on them. Pike kept going South West, the dyrection tha were coming from. Tha were scatered a long 2 or three miles. We could see them coming. We pushed on. [We] would meet a bunch all a long for a bout 2 miles. But we had no trouble with them. Pike had a little white flag in his hand all the way. He was trying to meet the chief. Every bunch we met would

[59]

try us on. Finaly we seen a big bunch coming an we met them. Tha made a stop an Pike stoped to. An the head chief motioned to Pike to come up. An tha met an shuck hands. An I was proud to see it.

An tha stoped rite thare, an it was no time til tha had a little wigwam streached an a little stick fire started rite in the midle of the little tent. Pike toald us to take off our sadles an bridles. An before we could hardly think tha cut our horses in the bunch, taken them off for the nite. Which I did not like.

Pike had some tobaco he gave to the oald chief. An when we got in the little tent Pike and the chief were smoking a big pipe. Tha would take 3 whifs an pass back an forth until tha smoked it out. An the chief filled up the pipe a gane an handed it to Pike, an he Pike taken 3 whifs an Wasatou—that was the chiefs name—motioned to Pike to pass it a round. Which he did, an we all smoked.[12]

While this was going a long, tha all begun to settle down for the nite. Tha began to come back an unload there packs. It was funey how tha done. I had to watch them camp. Tha would ride up an jump off of there poneys. The squaws would pull the blanket off there shoulders an unrap a little Indian kid and role

[12] This chief is probably unidentifiable. JLC calls him "Washington" at one point, perhaps confusing him with a Caddo chief named George Washington. On 12 August, at the Wichita agency, Pike made one treaty with four Comanche bands together and another the same day with the Wichita tribes and other agency Indians, but he also included, for some reason, a separate band of Comanches, the Peneteghcas (Penatekas). The names of several Comanche chiefs appear on each treaty, none of them similar to "Wasatou." A distant possibility is Tosawi, second chief of the Peneteghcas. *War of the Rebellion: Official Records of the Union and Confederate Armies*, 4th ser., 1 (Washington, D.C., 1900): 546, 554.

them out on the grass. I doant no how meney I seen. Some of them would crawl a bout on the grass, but tha did not look after them. I could not keep from watching them. Tha were a bout 3 thousand Indians in all, tha said. Doant no how long tha let there kids lay thare.

We looked wher we left our horses. We saw our sadles an bridles an ropes rite wher we left our horses. Tha had turned our horses in the herd an drove them off. So we drug our sadles an blankets in the little wigwam.

We begun to fix to eat our supper. Tha had lots of dride bufalo meat an fresh meat to. An we had bread an salt. The Indians did not eat bread nor use salt. We got some sticks, broild some of there fresh meat, but tha eat theres raw. So we dun fine. A long a bout 10 oclock every thing got still save the mounted camp gard. Tha were riding all nite, I think. I laid down but did not sleep mutch. I got a chance to speak to Pike. I toald him we had better watch very cloast that nite.

An he said, "Tha is no dainger, you are as safe here as you would be at home."

So I put my head on my sadle and lay down. Pike and oald Wasatou talked a great deal during the nite. I did not sleep mutch.

Tha began to git up a bout 4 oclock that morning. We eat breakfast, an Pike an Wasatou were talking. A bout sunup tha drove in there horses an led ours up, an we sadled them. Every thing was in confusion, or seamed to be. The Kiowa Indians was 8 or 10 miles South of us, an tha would not come in. Tha refused to treat with General Pike. Tha had made a big raid in the settlements on the Concho, drove out a big bunch of horses, an [the settlers] were foulowin them.[13] Pike thought tha could whip them into a treaty. My recolection is that oald Wasatou, head chief of the Comanche tribe, sent 400 of his picked warers with Pike to reinforce the men that were fighting [the Kiowas] out of the settlements. Oald Kickapoo Jo was there head chief. I think he was a white man from his looks. The Comanche Indians an Kiowas were fighting each other. The Comanche Indians had killed out the Kickapoo tribe, or nearly all of them. An oald Jo had worked in with the Kiowas an was the head chief.[14]

I doant no just what was dun. [Pike's bunch] cut in West [with] the others coming East, an [the Kiowas] had to fight out. [I don't know] whether it was General Carney or McCulloch that were [following and] fighting oald Jo.[15] But I will say tha fought like wild-

[13] At another place in the manuscript JLC writes that the settlers pursuing the Kiowas were from "near the Riogrand Valley." The raiders may have been returning from a foray into Mexico and struck at Texas settlements on the way home.

[14] Ordinarily the Comanches and the Kiowas were the closest of allies and had been for many years. According to Pike (who does not give an account of any battle in his report), the Kiowas quarreled with the Comanche bands who agreed to a treaty and threatened them along with the other tribes who complied. Pike, *Report*, 22–23. The Kickapoos, who were usually enemies of the Comanches, were far from extinct at this time. Rupert N. Richardson, *The Comanche Barrier to South Plains Settlement* (Glendale, Calif., 1933), 171, 230; James Farber, *Texas, C.S.A.* (New York, 1947), 219–20.

[15] No General Carney has been found in the records. Colonel, later General Henry E. McCulloch was authorized by the Secession Convention and later the Confederate government to raise a regiment of cavalry for defense of the northwest frontier of Texas against Indians. Troops from his command often joined with settlers to pursue marauding Indians. James Buckner Barry, *A Texas Ranger and Frontiersman: The Days of Buck*

cats. Tha fought all day off an on. Finaly [the Kiowas] made there big an last charge, an the boys said it was hot for a little while. I was not in on the mane big fight, but we lost sevrel men. One of my neighbors by the name of Jim Gibson was killed in the valley. Tha called it Lost Valley.[16] I doant no how meney Indians was killed, but tha finaly whiped them out, an tha scatterd all over the plaines like wolves.

We went on back to Fort Cobb with the Comanche Indians, a bout 3 thousand in all, an camped them on Beef Creek 2 or 3 miles East of Fort Cobb. Twitty an others fixed up the treaty with them. The state undertaken to feed them, feeding them on threw the summer. This was in July 61. I doant no where tha got the beef cattle. I helped herd the cattle. We held them on Beef Creek, about 3 miles East of the fort. When we began to kill beaves for the Indians, we would cut out 8 or 10 beaves a time an drive them to the slauter pen that the oald regulars used while tha were thare at Cobb. An it was a good one too. We would kill [beaves] every day an turn them over to [the Indians]. Tha would use the meat as tha pleased. We that was on herd would have to watch them cloast. Tha would try to cut out the cattle an scater the herd. Some of them was mean that way. But we would stand them off. We

Barry in Texas, 1845–1906, ed. James K. Greer (Dallas, 1932), 127ff; Rupert N. Richardson, *The Frontier of Northwest Texas, 1846–1876* (Glendale, Calif., 1963), 237–38; *Confederate Military History*, vol. 11, *Texas*, 42–43, 244–45.

[16] Apparently JLC is mistaken about the name of this valley. A battle about which he had no doubt heard took place in July 1874 in Lost Valley, Texas, between Kiowas and their allies under Lone Wolf and a detachment of Texas frontier rangers. Richardson, *Frontier*, 287; J. W. Wilbarger, *Indian Depredations in Texas* (Austin, 1889; reprint, 1967), 574–75.

did not haft to hurt eney of them. Tha would back off an leave.

Every evning tha was all wayes a bunch of squaws an mabe a hunderd or more kids a round the pen. An when we would kill a beef an take out the intrals an role out the ponch on the ground, it would be coverd with little Indians before you could think. An tha would pick it clean, eat it as tha picked it off, an keep plucking at it until the hole thing was eat up. Tha did not wash eney thing. Tha would pluck off the meat, eat it like wolves. The squaws would take the intrals an cary them off. Doant no what tha dun with them. Tha would clean every thing up, head an all.[17]

Every thing went smothe until a long in October or November, when tha got to breaking off in little squads an leavin the fort. Tha began to slip out an raid the settlements on the frontier of Texas. Tha finaly broke up an went on the war path.[18]

Before I go eney futher I want to relate a little sercumstance that ocurd while we were at Fort Cobb in the summer of 61. The Indians had made them some race tracks a bout one mile NW of the fort in the valley. Tha amused themselves by runing poney races every day. Tha had some good poneys too. I thought

[17] For a description of eating habits among the Comanches, see Ernest Wallace and E. Adamson Hoebel, *The Comanches: Lords of the South Plains* (Norman, Okla., 1952), 70–72.

[18] Submitting his report to the Confederate government at just about the time that this Comanche departure was taking place, Pike spoke a great deal of the terms he had agreed upon with the Indians, some of them so generous that President Davis recommended against them in handing on the report to the Confederate congress. Pike was overoptimistic about the behavior of the Comanches encamped near Fort Cobb and believed by the time he wrote that even the recalcitrant Kiowas were ready to submit. Pike, *Report*, 3–5, 23; Richardson, *Comanche Barrier*, 270–71.

my horse could out run eney thing tha had, boy like. So I sliped off one morning an went out to the tracks by myself. Tha were 4 to 5 hunderd Indians thare. Tha were runing races. I rode up, went out on the tracks. An in no time tha sent a good looking poney out an made motions to run, an in a fiew minutes we matched a race. Tha put a little Indian on there poney, an I rode my horse. The way tha run, tha make a long mark at each end of the tracks an make the horses toe the mark at the start. Then the one that crossed the mark first at the outcome wone the race.[19]

I had found an oald officers coat at the fort that had some brass aplets on the sholders. Tha were brite an shiney as gold. I put up the sholder straps againce a poney.

Them oald Indians would pat me on the sholders an say, "Him heap boy." An the little Indian boy was gigling an lafing an snigrin at me all the time, until we started. Tha were a big oald Indian held stakes. We had to ride up to the far end of the tracks to start. Tha was a fiew went with us. Me an the boy toed the mark an turned our horses in a run without a word. He got the start on me but I past him the first hunderd yards. He was whiping, but I run out a head 4 or 5 steps, run rite off an left his poney, come out a way a head. An as soon as I rode back to the poles, here come the oald Indian with the poney an the aplets, as tha were called. Handed me the rope an pated me on the back an said, "Heap boy." So you see, tha was

---

[19] For comments on the Comanche's fondness for horse racing, see Richardson, *Comanche Barrier*, 43.

some honor in the Indians in that respect. Tha looked my horse all over and pated me on the sholder an said, "Heap boy." An in no time tha brung up a nother horse an we was a bout to make a nother race. I was beting the poney I wone an the aplets againce a good horse. A bout the time we got ready to run, up rode our lieutenant, Sam Miller, an orderd me under arest. The capton [had sent him] an Tom Sullivan an John Lynch after me. Tha come an capturd me an that settled the race. Tha made me leave the poney, an all taken me to head quarters to Capton Twitty. He was pretty hot, an gave me a good talk, told me to stay a way from the Indians, as it was daingerous to be a bout them at eney time. An said if I ever disobade orders an run off a gane, he would cort marshel me an have me shot. That broke up my horse racing with the Indians.

If tha had let me alone, I woulda wone a herd of poneys, because I had a good horse.

[When these Indians went on the warpath in the fall of 1861,] the first thing tha dun was to murder Coatneys famley. Tha lived not very far South of the fort. [The Indians] killed one of his children an went on, I doant no wher. Coatney left with his famley at once. He had a farm an good hued log houses. We went out after the Indians but tha were gone when we got thare, had tore up the place an tride to burn the houses. So we did not stay [at the fort] mutch longer. We left one evning an rode in the nite. I doant no how far. We found sevrel ricks of millet that had been put up by some men. Tha had camped thare. We [had

seen] them sowing the millet as we past going from
Arbuckle to Fort Cobb. The Indians foulowed us an
tride to stampede our horses while tha were eating
the millet. Tha thought we would camp thare, but the
order was to take the bits out of our horses mouths an
not take off our sadles. [The Indians] crawld up grunt-
ing like hogs, an S. H. Miller our lieutenant shot one
of them. An he run like a wolf. Doant no how bad he
was hurt.

But we left an came on to Elem Springs on the
Washita before we stoped to camp an git eney thing to
eat. We came on to Gainesville, I think in one day
an nite, as well as I remember. Doant no what time in
the nite.

But I got leaf to go home with the under standing that I would report at Camp Reeves in Grayson
Co. We was orderd [there] for the purpose of being
organised in the Confederate service.

We all reported at Camp Reeves, remained thare
for sevrel dayes. Doant no what tha were waiting for.
My father did not want me in Confederate service, so
before we were sworn in [he] got a man by the name
of George Williams to take my place in the company.[20]
I was paid off in state scrip. I think tha paid me $40 or

[20] Young's regiment was taken into Confederate service as the Eleventh Texas Cavalry. At this time, or perhaps later, JLC's company acquired
a new commanding officer, for William Twitty remained in Gainesville.
War of the Rebellion, 1st ser., vol. 22, pt. 2, 799; Diamond, "Account," 352;
Gunter Papers, 223. The regiment went on to see action in several battles
from Arkansas east, commanded for a time by Colonel James J. Diamond
after Young's death in 1862. *Confederate Military History*, vol. 11, *Texas*, 47,
51, 130, 166–67; Harry McCorry Henderson, *Texas in the Confederacy* (San
Antonio, 1955), 128.

50<u>00</u> in scrip. It was not worth mutch at that time. I doant no how mutch Father paid George Williams but he paid him some thing.

But I came home with Pap. I could have quit without eney subestatute on a count of my age. I was onely a bout 17 or 18 years old. But Father did not no.

Capton Bob Bean of Gainesville knew Williams awful well. I think Williams belonged to his company. He said that George was killed, I think at Corinth in a battle with the Federals.[21]

The company stade at Camp Reeves in Grayson Co. I came home an stade until the spring of 62. A man by the name of John T. Crisp came to Gainesville with his fathers famley. His fathers name was Green Crisp, an a strong Union man, an badley tore up. So John T. Crisp made up a company in Gainesville in earley spring of 62, to go to John T. Coffee in Missouri. He Coffee had a regiment of state gards in Missouri.[22] Crisp was my mothers cousin. An he told Father if I would go with him he would take me to my Uncle Jack Hicklin, who lived in Newton County, Missouri.[23] Coffee an Shelby an the Crisps were related, an the Hicklins all so. Uncle Jack Hicklin oned a bout

[21] Robert Bean was a pioneer settler in Cooke County. Jones, *Early Days*, 26–27. The Eleventh Texas Cavalry was in the region of Corinth by May 1862. The culminating battle there took place on 3–4 October 1862. *Confederate Military History*, vol. 11, *Texas*, 160–63.

[22] Colonel John T. Coffee recruited a sizable force in the Jackson County region of Missouri in the spring and summer of 1862, even though most of the area was nominally behind Union lines. By mid-August he was moving southward with other recruiters ahead of advancing Union forces. *Confederate Military History*, vol. 9, *Missouri*, 98–99.

[23] An Uncle John Hicklin is mentioned near the end of this account as having been a member of Quantrill's band of Confederate guerrillas. Whether he is the same as Jack Hicklin has not been ascertained.

600 slaves. Tha said his place looked like a city. Tha were sevrel men went with Crisp to git to the north.

Crisp finaly got to Pineville, Missouri an found every thing in confusion. Shelby was [farther up] in Mo. recruiting an tha had put General Hindman in command of the western division of the armey. He orderd Coffee to organise in the Confederate service, an he refused to do so. An Hindman had his regiment at Pineville.[24]

Crisp tuck his company out North of town an camped to wait for Shelby. He made us a talk an toald us if eney of us wanted to go on North to ride off. An Ellison Skaggs an Frank Huckle an Jack Harrison rode off North. Crisp repeated a gane.

I stayd with Crisp to go to Uncle Jack Hicklins. Crisp tole me not to go, that he would make his word good.

I wish Father had gone North with Crisp. If he had, that bloody handed Bourland mob would not a murderd him. But the Devel got the most of them, an if tha is eney of the mob left, the Devel got them branded good an deep. Tha caint shed it off.[25]

Now we had to stay a fiew dayes until Shelby come.

[24] After the Battle of Pea Ridge in March 1862 most of the units in Arkansas were ordered east of the Mississippi for reinforcements around Corinth. Among them was a company under then Captain Joseph O. Shelby. He was back in Arkansas by June with authorization to recruit a regiment, which he proceeded to do in southern Missouri. *Confederate Military History*, vol. 9, *Missouri*, 97, 221–22. General Thomas Hindman was given command of the Confederate department west of the Mississippi in May 1862. He was relieved of that command in July because of his severe methods of building an army, but when he was assigned to a lesser territory, he went on organizing with a heavy hand in western Arkansas. *Confederate Military History*, vol. .10, *Arkansas*, 105–20, 129, 403–404.

[25] See Editor's Introduction.

General Hindman apointed a man by the name of Crawford over Coffees regiment. An I doant no wher Coffee was, as I did not have eney thing to say in the matter. But when Shelby come, him an Crisp made a change all a round. Shelby an Crisp claimed that Hindman had no rite to apoint a cornel over the regiment, that the solgers had the rite to elect there cornel. So we put a man by the name of Thompson in as cornel, an we elected all of our officers in the regiment. I doant no what become of Crawford when tha nocked him out. Shelby was apointed brigadier general.[26]

We were orderd to Cross Hollows, Arkansas from Pineville. But the Cane Hill fight had all ready come off when we got thare. We went from thare to Newtonia, Mo. We stade thare at Hazel Springs until the Newtonia fight came off in the late summer or fall of 62. It was a lively 2 dayes fight. The Rebles whiped them the first day. The Federals retreated North, an we held the town an stade thare on the ground 2 dayes. The 3 day tha came a gane. Tha had reinforced. Tha had 2 to one but we gave them a good little fight very near all day. General Cooper and Stand Watie had got in the ring with Shelby an Marmaduke.[27]

[26] The Crawford appointed by General Hindman has not proved to be traceable. When Coffee was relieved of his command, he is said to have been replaced by Colonel Gideon W. Thompson. *Confederate Military History*, vol. 9, *Missouri*, 99, 103. This officer had recruited a body of cavalry in the same area of Missouri in which Coffee had recruited and fought beside his and other units as they withdrew south, with enough men to form three regiments. Shelby was given command of a brigade of these troops. He was not promoted to brigadier general until near the end of 1863. *Confederate Military History*, vol. 9, *Missouri*, 98–100; ibid., vol. 10, *Arkansas*, 131–32.

[27] The Battle of Newtonia began on 30 September 1862, after a

But tha were too strong for us, an we fell back South near Batesville, Arkansas. Remained there a short time, an Shelby an Marmaduke made a raid up in Missouri, went as far as Cape Girardeau.[28]

We rode 5 or 6 dayes an a good part of the nite, had a little fight at Patsonville, tuck the outfit with a lot of comasarys an some prisnors, went on to Fredericktown, tuck that little outfit with comasarys, an some prisnors, rushed on to Girardeau on the Mississippi River, stoped at oald Jackson, Missouri a bout 10 miles East from Girardeau an fed our horses an ourselves, as we was jaded down badley.

An Marmaduke divided the armey an toald

---

buildup of the armies on both sides. *Confederate Military History*, vol. 9, *Missouri*, 100–101; ibid., vol. 10; *Arkansas*, 131–32. All the officers spoken of here were Confederate colonels, later generals. Douglas H. Cooper, district commander of the Indian Territory, arrived with three to four thousand Indians and Texans on 27 September and assumed command as the ranking officer present. His prewar work as a United States Indian agent and other service had brought him honorary membership in the Chickasaw tribe. Stand Watie, a prominent Cherokee and a firm supporter of the Confederacy, led his Cherokee Mounted Rifles through many engagements in the Civil War and is said to have been the last southern general to surrender. Rampp and Rampp, *Civil War*, 179–80 passim. John S. Marmaduke, a West Pointer and an experienced officer, was selected by General Hindman as commander of a brigade of the newly arrived Missouri volunteers and also of a cavalry division made up of his own brigade, the one under Shelby, and another under a Colonel Bradfute. *Confederate Military History*, vol. 9 *Missouri*, 100; ibid., vol. 10, *Arkansas*, 134. JLC is mistaken in placing the date of the Battle of Cane Hill before that of Newtonia. The Cane Hill fight occurred in December 1862. Ibid., vol. 9, *Missouri*, 104–106.

[28] JLC was at Camp Porter, near Batesville, for longer than he remembered. He wrote a letter from there to his family in Texas on 20 March 1863 (see p. 116). The Marmaduke-Shelby raid into Missouri that he goes on to describe began in mid-April 1863 and continued through a difficult withdrawal back into Arkansas in late May. *Confederate Military History*, vol. 9, *Missouri*, 130–34; ibid., vol. 10, *Arkansas*, 165; Robert L. Kerby, *Kirby Smith's Confederacy: The Trans-Mississippi South, 1863–1865* (New York, 1972), 125–27.

Shelby to go on to Cape Girardeau, the fort, an wait a bout half way. An he Marmaduke would take the most of the men a round South. An for Shelby to wait for orders before he atacted the place. But as soon as Marmaduke left, Shelby formed us in a howlo square an made a talk, an said he beleaved that General Marmaduke had wetted on our face, [his] march would a mount to no thing. An said he Shelby was in favor of fighting them eney way. An we would advance on to Cape Girardeau, an for us to folow him.

Marmaduke [had] left the train an the canon with Shelby. So we went on with the hole outfit, got in a bout 2 miles of Girardeau, the fort, an left the train. Taken the canon a bout a mile east of the fort an opend fire with 12 guns. It was called the Bledsoe Battery.[29] Shelby sent a bout 4 or 5 hunderd men a round North of the canon, an tha were to charge when orderd. I was detailed to cary dispaches from one to the other.

In a short time the Federals come out with in a bout ½ mile of our line an turned loos on us. An the limbs began to fall off of them blackjack trees. An our boys were handing it back to [them]. Things got pretty hot.

An Marmaduke come with his men an orderd Shelby under arest for disobaying orders, an orderd a

[29] The unit mentioned here was Captain Joseph Bledsoe's Missouri battery of horse artillery, a segment of Shelby's brigade. The battery saw action in most of the battles that JLC mentions, among them Marmaduke's first cavalry raid into Missouri in January 1863. JLC does not say whether he went along on the earlier raid. Kerby, *Kirby Smith*, 36; *Confederate Military History*, vol. 9, *Missouri*, 101; ibid., vol. 10, *Arkansas*, 138, 153.

retreat. An I had to cary the dispach. An as I went I could see the Federal line coming out of the fort. Tha were shooting at us from the gunboats. I am here to say canon balles were coming thick all a round til we got a way, went back to oald Jackson the way we come. The Federals kept rite on our heales, would fire on the rear gard every once in a while. An tha would have a little spat.

But we kept going all nite. The next day tha held up a while an we got some thing to eat an feed our horses. But not long. We would stop an fight them when tha got too cloast, an then go on South. For 3 or 4 dayes tha would flank us on both sides. Tha had a bout 4 to 1 of us.

Finaly we got to the Saint Francis River, an it was up a big rise. An tha thought tha had us hemed. But Marmaduke an Shelby stoped [in] a bout 2 miles of the river an formed a line on a divide at a little town tha called Bloomfield, an opend fire on them when tha got cloast anuff. Shelby [had] put men to work choping timber down, throwing it every way for a breast work. [The Federals] came up an found what was dun. Tha moved South an formed a line, an our battery opend fire a gane. An tha begun to shoot at our line. [Then] the Federals sent a part of there force a round North of our armey to make a charge on us. An tha aimed to keep advancing from the East. So there wing made a charge, an swoped down on us rite in the little town. An tha were shooting from the East with there canon. An shells was coming thick an fast. We were orderd to dismount in short order, an in counting off it fell on me to hold horses—I hapend to be the 4 man.[30] Just as we dismounted a shell exploded rite under our horses heads, an I was holding 4. An one of them jumped on me an nocked me down an broke my ancle.

But [the Federals] soon got anuff of us, an tha fell back. When tha struck the breast works we made it hot for them.

So boath sides got down to business for 4 or 5 hours. The fight lasted until nite. There general got killed. His name was McNeil, tha said.[31] An tha ceased firing. Everything luld down a bout sundown. We still held the ground until we sliped out after dark.

Shelby had sent men with our horses an swam the river. But we did not no of it until after dark, when we was orderd to fall in to line an sliped off on the march. Tha had made a floting bridge a cross the river that we could cross on a fiew at a time. We finaly all got a cross an found our horses. Tha had swum them by companys at a time an kept them seperated by regiments. So we got our horses without eney trouble. Tha crossed the canon at the last with out eney trouble, roled the wagones a cross by hand an cut the bridge loos an let it go down the river.

The Federals foulowed us to the river next morn-

---

[30] See Editor's Introduction, p. 18 n. 1.

[31] Brigadier General John McNeil, Union commander of the Rolla district in Missouri, had hanged ten Confederate guerrillas on the Palmyra courthouse square in October 1862. The Confederate officers wanted very much to capture him on this foray but did not succeed in doing so. If some general was killed in the battle, it was not McNeil. The rumor that he was a casualty may have sprung from wishful thinking. Kerby, *Kirby Smith*, 45; *Confederate Military History*, vol. 9, *Missouri*, 131–33; ibid., vol. 10, *Arkansas* 163, 165.

ing an fired on us, an [we] fired back at them. But tha turned back.

We went on to Batesville, Arkansas. Then we stoped an tuck a little rest an sent the prisnors to Little Rock, Arkansas. I was on the detail to take them an turn them over. We stade thare a fiew dayes an was orderd back to our company. The company had been orderd to Dardanelle, Arkansas, on the river.

As we came back we met a little squad of solgers, an tha had 2 of our company under gard taking them to Little Rock. Tha boath were my neighbors. One was by the name of O. B. Atkinson, the other by the name of Jim Davidson. Tha had got away from the Bourland mob that was here in Gainesville, Texas in the fall of 62, an had come to our company an never told eney thing as to what was going on here.[32] If tha had told eney thing, the mob would have had some thing to do when tha met us. Tha toald some thing [now], a bout the murder, but tha did not no mutch, as tha got a way at the start. Tha boath had sined the paper. Here is the substanc of the request that [the signers] were making. It will be remembered that in the Spring of 62 the Confederate Congress pased what tha called an exzemtion law to exzemp every

[32] Probably Atkinson and Davidson were the two men whose escape Barrett reports. Obediah B. Atkinson was an early settler in Cooke County. He patented land there in 1857. JLC identifies him as the organizer of the Union League. Atkinson and Davidson were no doubt among the men with whom Frederick Sumner was imprisoned in Little Rock from January to August, 1863. Sumner, also a member of the league, fled Sherman, Texas, just ahead of the Confederate military at the time of the crackdown, only to be arrested in Arkansas on suspicion of Union involvement. Barrett, *Hanging*, 12; Cooke County Records, Book 4, p. 564; *Frank Leslie's Illustrated Newspaper* (New York), 20 February 1864; see p. 95.

man from military service that oned as meney as ten slaves. An a man by the name of McNutt got up a petison to the Confederate congress to remove that law. An these men that were murderd had put there names on the petison, claiming a slaveholder had no rite to be exzemted.

So we went on to join our company. But on our way the man that had charg of us found out some how that tha had Crisp, our capton, under gard at Russellville, not far from Dardanelle, wher our company was. When we learned that we turned for Russellville in quick time.

When we got thare we found our capton thare under gard. Tha was some big ikes watching him. Tha toald us we could not talk to him then. He was upstares, I think in a hotel. We never paid eney atension to what tha said. We had as meney men as tha had.

So [the man that had charge of us] walked rite in an we stood by. An the capton talked to us an said for us to go on to Dardanelle to the company. An for us to camp rite on the bank of the river so we could not be surrounded. An to watch every movement. An if eney thing came up to be reddy. An not give up to a thousand men. Just shoot it out. The capton never said eney thing about the murdering of 44 good men for there Union princables by the mob.

We come on an toald the boys an our lieutenant Bob Moore what the capton said. An we made a raid on the ordnance store that nite. Capton Brown was in charge of the comasery. We tuck all the amanition an sevrel armey muskets.

As soon as Shelby got the word he sent Crisp

back to his company. We come very near going to Russellville the day tha relesed Crisp, but Moore made a talk, [and] we put it off one day longer.

Rite at that time [when] I found out what was [happening] down here in Gainesville, I said I would not fight for eney government that would tolerate as bloody crimes as that. Of corse this Bourland gang had reported a pack of lies, or tha would not have arested Crisp our capton. No telling what tha had reported.[33]

Now as to that Bourland mob, tha was not mutch danger in them, onely when tha got some oald men tied, then tha would murder them most brutaly. But tha were a cowrdly gang wanting to keep out of the armey. Shelby said if he had nown eney thing a bout what tha were doing here in Gainesville, he would a sent a regiment here and killed the hole D out fit, an sent the oald men home to there famleys.

When Crisp come, [the company] went to the regiment. Tha were at Cross Hollows, Arkansas. Marmaduke and Shelby was orderd to Helena on the Mississippi River. We fought that battle and got whiped, fell back in Arkansas.[34] Then [we were] orderd to Little Rock, or the Arkansas Post, to fight a big battle there. That was in the summer of 63.[35]

---

[33] JLC first heard of the Gainesville lynchings in November 1862 and by 2 January 1863 had received a letter from his mother informing him that his father had been among the victims. A contradiction of loyalties is evident in his reply, but this letter is not in his handwriting or in his usual style, and the friend or scribe who wrote it may have relied now and then on stock phrases. See p. 114.

[34] The Battle of Helena was fought on 3 and 4 July 1863. *Confederate Military History*, vol. 9, *Missouri*, 134–35; ibid., vol. 10, *Arkansas*, 176–93.

[35] The "big battle" shaping up at this time was the struggle between

On the way thare, me an John D. Powers rode off one morning from near Bayou Meto, north of Little Rock.[36] Crisp helped us some by giving us a pass to foulow one of our company mules that we claimed had got a way that nite. Crisp rote the pass, an we went to head quarters, an the agent general sined it. So we was safe for 3 dayes. That give us a good start. Of corse we had to here of the mule all a long. We had some trouble with the malisha once or twiste. But if we could not [lie] out we would fight out. Tha [had] hung John Powers brother in Gainesville, an we were boath determined to come home. We were very well armed, had some trouble at Mount Ida, Ark, cross Red River north of Paris, Texas. Had some trouble thare with the malisha, or heal flies, as we called them.[37]

Me an John D. Powers got [to Gainesville] an found our foalks here at home. So we concluded to join Mains Co, Bourland regiment. Tha were stationed at Montague town, Montague Co. So we went an talked to Bourlands agent general in Gainesville. His name was Whaley. An he said we had a rite to stay on the frontier an help keep the Indians out of the

Union and Confederate armies for possession of Little Rock. The battle took place in the latter part of August and the first ten days of September, after JLC had deserted and headed for Texas. *Confederate Military History*, vol. 9, *Missouri*, 136–39; ibid., vol. 10, *Arkansas*, 208–22.

[36] Bayou Meto rises in the hills north of Little Rock and flows southeast, emptying into the Arkansas River. The town of Bayou Meto stands on its east bank, not far from the juncture with the Arkansas. JLC's company was encamped near the river close to Little Rock, not near the town. He must have left his company in late July or early August. The problem of desertion from the Confederate army was severe in this area at the time. *Confederate Military History*, vol. 10, *Arkansas*, 208; Kerby, *Kirby Smith*, 220.

[37] Farber, *Texas, C.S.A.*, 184.

settlements. So we went an joined Mains company—
that was in the late summer of 63—remained with
the company til a bout the last of March or first of
April 64.[38]

During the time I was in Capton Mains company,
I was scouting all the time on the frontiers of Texas.
Had sevrel spats with the Indians. I will give one fight
that we had at Illinois Bend on Red River in the fall of
63, October I think. Mains sent a little bunch of us out
to a little fort to watch for Indians an gard a fiew famleys that lived on the river. Taylor Cummings was in
charge of the outfit. He was first sargent of our company. The famleys that lived a round cloast come in
an forted up. We watched cloast for Indians or there
trailes. Tha were sliping in every light moon.

Every thing run smoth for a fiew dayes. Finaly
one day me an a man by the name of Bill Gwynn crost
the river at the bend, went over in the Territory, as it
was called then, now Oklahoma. We went up Mud
Creek to what was called Flag Springs looking for
dear. Gwynn was raised on the frontier, an not afraid
an a little careless. [We] hadnt went far north of the
springs til Gwynn shot a mity fine buck. He would
[always] take his oald rifle a long. So he killed it in its
tracks. He went to load a gane an got the bullet partly

[38] Colonel James Bourland was a long term citizen of Texas and, like
many other Cooke County leaders in that day, a planter in the Red River
bottom. During most of the Civil War he commanded the Texas Frontier
Regiment, whose chief task was to protect frontier settlers from marauding Indians. The Whaley who is called Bourland's adjutant general was
probably L. F. Whaley. No information has been found about a Captain
Mains. Smith, *First 100 Years*, 43; Jones, *Early Days*, 10; Kerby, *Kirby Smith*,
216; Barry, *Texas Ranger*, 168, 237.

down an broke his gun stick. An was making a nother when my horse raised his head an snorted. An I toald Gwynn tha were Indians a round cloast.

He laught at me an said, "Lem, you are all wayes finding Indians."

An a bout the time he spoke tha had us surrounded an was shooting at us all a round. An we did not wait to be told to git out. We never fired a gun at them. I was riding a good horse an Gwynn was riding a poney. I threw my old musket down on one of [the Indians]—I had a cut off musket I all wayes caried to the horne of my sadle with a strap. The Indian was rushing rite on us, but he stoped at once. Tha thought we would run south down Mud Creek. But we went West, clum the bluff, went out on the high prery, struck the bluff on the river. We knew the trail way to a crossing. When we got to the river the Indians were coming down the bluff as fast [as] tha could. When we struck the water Gwynn jumped off his poney, went down the river, toald me to go on, as his poney was give out. The river was down, so I got a cross all rite. Doant no whether tha foulowed me or not. The last I seen of them tha were coming down the bluff. I did not look back after I struck the water. But Gwynns poney foulowed me a cross the river. I finaly got to the fort an reported to Taylor, as we called him, an he went to wher we first saw [the Indians]. Seen lots of sine but no Indians. He could not report Indians until tha were in Texas.

So the next morning he tuck all his men on the river to see if tha could find wher tha crossed the river. Left me an Gwynn at the fort, as we was sorter

Left: Only surviving portrait of Nathaniel Miles Clark, made about 1860. *Right:* Mahuldah Hicklin Clark (1820–83), widow of Nathaniel Miles Clark, in the 1870s.

Nathaniel Miles Clark's log cabin, built in 1857 on his original homestead of 160 acres seven miles southeast of Gainesville, Texas. It was in use as a barn when this photograph was made in the 1920s, and it burned in the early 1930s.

James Lemuel Clark and his wife, Mary Ann Thomas Clark (1845–1913), about 1900.

Clark homeplace, 1905. Mary Ann and James Lemuel are in the center foreground. The others are three of their children: Jimmie Cordelia on the porch and, in the buggy, Thomas Hicklin (*left*) and Josephus (*right*).

James Lemuel Clark and two of his grandchildren, Iva Nettie Clark and L. D. Clark, in 1925.

James Lemuel Clark and his sister, Cordelia Ann Clark Waggoner (1845–1933), about 1930.

Gravestone of Nathaniel Miles Clark, erected in 1878. Note
that the year of his birth is given incorrectly as 1816 instead
of 1818. (Photograph by Michael Clark)

tired from our run. An about twelve oclock one of the Anderson boys come an woke me up. I had laid down on a load of corne in the shade to take a nap.

He said, "Look at the Indians coming."

I looked down East of the fort, an shur anuff tha were a bout one hunderd [of them].

A man by the name of Hatfield lived 2 or 3 hunderd yards East of the fort with his wife an children. Tha was all coming in a hury towards the fort. Tha were only me an Lock Foster an Gwynn to fight them off, an old man Andersons famley, an old man Willets famley, an Hatfields famley. The Indians were coming rite a long with Hatfields famley, cuting all sorts of shines, an Hatfield standing them off, him an his brother. Lock thought best to let Hatfield advise, an stay with him, as he was a Californian an a Indian fighter. So I loped down an met them an toald Hatfield what we wanted. An one of the Indians made a run on me. I pulled down on him, an he got anuff. I run back to the fort, an [then I saw] Hatfields hole outfit were gone an hid in the brush some wher. An Gwynn dun the same, left me an Lock Foster there with the women an children. Oald man Willet was sick with tyfoid an newmonia. He [was] very bad off. Oald man Anderson was oald an feble. John Willet was gone after Dr Gordon for his father.[39]

[The Indians] had Taylor Cummings an the boys cut off from the fort, an owing to old man Willet being sick, me an Lock toald them to all git in the

---

[39] While the dates of the two accounts do not agree, this Indian raid is clearly the one described in Smith, *First 100 Years*, 40–43. The dates given there are 21–23 December 1863.

cabin wher the oald man was, an we would dismount an fight them off. This was all in quick time, as tha had the little fort surrounded all the time.

So tha came like a storm rite on us, shooting and yelling. It was like a thunder storm. Me an Lock dismounted at the dore to run in to the cabin, an met the women an children an oald man Willet all in a hudle coming out. The oald man had his gun an shot at them. Doant no whether oald man Anderson shot or not. Tha all run West to a little gate that was at the West end of the row of cabins. Tha run East an West all mixed up. Tha were all scart to death. Could not do eney thing with them. So me an Lock finaly got on our horses an fought our waye threw. Before we got to this gate, tha were all runing in every direction. Me an Lock an the Indians were all mixed up to geather an was doing some good running. We went West, the Montague road. When we come threw this gate I speak of, behind women [and] children, Mandy Willet grabed at Lock Fosters bridle reighns. We run the road a bout half [a] mile an turned South rite in the breaks of Mountain Creek. Tha run us a bout 3 or 4 miles before tha turned back. The last we seen of them, tha were a bout 2 or 3 hunderd yards behind us.

We went on to Capton Gwynns. He lived a bout 2 miles North of the Head of Elem, as we called it then, now Saint Jo.[40] Every body forted up at the Head of Elem at once. Me an Lock went on to Montague to report to Capton Mains. When we got thare Capton

[40] The town was first called Head of Elm because the Elm Fork of the Trinity River had its source in large springs nearby.

[82]

Rowlands company were thare.[41] Tha had fought the Indians that morning on Little Wichita, an were foulowing [them]. So me an Lock went on with the little force to the Head of Elem, stade til morning. We overtaken [the Indians] on Dry Elem. Tha were going towards Gainesville. Tha were in what was called the Potter Field. Oald man Potter had fenced sevrel hunderd acres in pasture, taken in the creek, with rails. When the Indians saw us, tha went threw the East string of the fence in to the bottom an got in the brush. Rowland made a charge on them. When we came to the fence the capton told us to all dismount an throw the rails in, an leave the corners for breast workes. Which we did, for a bout ¼ mile, an we went after them in a hury. Hadnt went far when tha come on us every direction. But tha soon sorter stoped. We fell back to the fence, got behind the corners an begun to shoot. An tha got a way in a hury.

Tha went South down Dry Elem, crossed Big Elem at the mouth of Brushy Elem. Rowland knew tha had a bout 2 to 1.

We stade with [Rowlands company] when tha went to the fort. Tha found oald man Willet dead with a arow in his head. Tha found oald man Anderson dead a little ways off. [The Indians] had most

---

[41] John T. Rowland's company was Company D, Mounted Regiment, Texas State Volunteers. The efficiency and loyalty of this company, similar in most ways to the one to which JLC belonged, was called into question late in the war. One source has it that Rowland's company and others of the regiment were taken into Confederate service on 1 January 1864. Smith, *First 100 Years*, 43; Barry, *Texas Rangers*, 169–71; Strong, *His Memoirs*, 30ff.

brutaly murderd Mandy Willet, an she was not very far from the old man, her dady. Tha [had] taken the oald lady Anderson East of the rest, an her little baby, an killed them. Tha cut her breast off, boath of them, killed the baby againce a tree like you would kill a rabbit. The oald lady Willet an her oaldest daughter, tha sliped out some how an run an hid on the little branch that runs South of the fort. An stade all nite, not noing tha were boath thare til next morning when tha come out. Tha were hid cloast to geather in the bed of the creek.

Tha brought the dead bodys to the Head of Elem. I doant no wher tha buried them.

We never could overtake the Indians. Tha out run us, as our horses were run down. When we crossed Big Elem I went to the company at Montague an got leave from Capton Mains to come home for 10 dayes.

[Then I] went back an went to oald Mabel Gilberts a bout half way from Montague town on the Head of Elem, as tha were some famleys forted up thare. Mains sent me an Morris Gilbert an Rufus Renner an Perry McCool out thare as a gard. We stade thare a while an went back to the company. Tha all broke up. The most of them went to Montague town.

Every thing went smoth until February 64, when the Indians made a nother raid on the settlement an come as far as Red River Station in Montague County. Tha hapend to be sevrel of us at the station at the time. Oald Wilson Fletcher was in charge of us. We over tuck the Indians after a run for a bout 5 miles. Before we come on them, we met a little bunch of setlers after them. Pole Milam was in the bunch that was after them. We had a little spat an tha scaterd in the breaks an got a way.

I went back to the company, stade a fiew dayes, an was sent out on a nother scout up on the river, about 15 of us. Dr Armstrong was in charge of us, as he was our 2 lieutenant. We were sevrel dayes. We stade at Queen Peak a while, west of Montague town. We were on the eave of going North, was a bout reddy to make the start. We were going to Fort Gibson in the Indian Nation then, as the Federals were thare.[42]

Tha were some of our men that was with us had some trouble. Tha had a shooting scrape at the Head of Elem in 61, 2 or 3 killed in the fray, fell out over the war. The whole company or near a bout it were Union men. An Bourland sent a company of his bloody hands thare to arest the whole company, an tha come an taken in the outfit an put a gard all a round the town.[43]

That was late one evning. Tha got Dave Cooley, one of our company, an tied him to a tree an shot him all to peaces. Claimed that he killed Dan Brumley at the Head of Elem in the little fight tha had in 61. Luke Brumley was with them.

So you can see what kind of men some of the Bourland men were.

[42] The federals had retaken Fort Gibson in October 1862 but soon had to withdraw. They were again in possession of it by January 1863 and held it from then on, despite repeated attempts by the Confederates to capture it. Kerby, *Kirby Smith*, 42, 122.

[43] The prospect of being incorporated again into the Confederate army surely had much to do with the desertion of JLC and others like him. Bourland's Frontier Regiment and other such units were charged with keeping down desertions, a task that became increasingly difficult as many saw that the days of the Confederacy were numbered. Farber, *Texas, C.S.A.*, 218; Barry, *Texas Ranger*, 156, 171ff., 201; Richardson, *Frontier*, 244–46.

We were coming in that evning. Got to the pub-lick well a bout a half mile from town an met Joe Boydsons wife. She had crawled all the way to wait for us. An tha were women sliped threw in every direc-tion. We wanted to make a charge on them. Boydson was with us, an as brave a man as ever lived. But his wife wanted us to go on North. Which we did. She was a brave an smart little woman.

I am satisfide tha knew we were at the well, 8 or 10 of us in the bunch, because we stade some time at the well. Some of the boys wanted to make a charge on the outfit, but the women said if we did go to shooting we mite kill women and children. So we finaly sent runers out to geather up the boys that wanted to go North with us. Tha were on Denton Creek in the brush.

We went to Queen Peak in Montague County and stade thare a while an recruited up to a bout 20 men. Charles O. Davis an his bunch fell in at the Peak. We went on towards Jacksboro, an when we got thare the company had busted up an all left the place, every thing tore up an scaterd over the prery for 2 or 3 miles. Tha went South aiming to go to Mexico. We thought tha were going with us, but tha left before we got thare. I knew some of the men that were in there outfit: oald Martin Neely an Joe Lowe an others from Jacksboro.[44]

We went West to Secret Springs in Clay County. Thare we stade one day waiting for recruites. Tha come up a bout nite, an we numberd 37 men. We

[44] Martin Neely appears to have been the first resident of Cooke County, arriving in 1845. Smith, *First 100 Years*, 6.

elected our capton. We put Charles O. Davis in for capton, an made a good selection. We had scouts behind 4 or 5 miles watching. We knew tha would foulow us.

We went on West, crost [the] Pease River a bout where Vernon is now, went on West up Red River in order to go a round the Comanche Indians country, sometimes on one side an the other. I doant no how far we did travle up the river before we turned North, I gess a bout 100 miles. West of oald Fort Cobb, we turned North East aiming to go to Fort Gibson, as the Union army were thare at that time.

We got in a desert dry strip of country an got pretty hungry an thirsty, on [the] South Canadian an the Salt Fork, a bove the mouth of each one. [We] went on NE an crost the Arkansas River at what is called the Rock Ford. Went on an struck the Verdigris about 50 miles North West of Fort Gibson. Thare we found wiled hogs an some catle an game of all kinds. Went down the Verdigris to the main Fort Scott an Fort Gibson road, crost at the Alberta Stand.

Of corse tha was not eney body living at there homes. Some fine houses an good farmes all threw the country. But the Indians had split up. Some went North an some South, an one side would not let the other side stay. Tha called the Indians that went North the Pin Indians, an them that went South the Pins called Secesh. An tha would kill each other eney time tha got the chance. It dun them Pins good to kill a Butternut, as tha called them.[45]

[45] According to Albert Pike, long before secession a "pin" society had existed among the Indians. It was a secret organization whose members

So we stade at the Alberta houses one day an nite. Tha was a little store house or 2 a bout ¼ of a mile North of the mane house, an 2 white men dead in one of them. Had been dead sevrel dayes. We had no way to bury them, so we had to let them a lone.

The next day we taken the road South towards Fort Gibson an travled a bout 5 miles an met the Federals, a bout 5 or 6 hunderd, on the way to Fort Scott, Kansas. Tha taken us for bushwhackers. We was a hard looking outfit. But Davis our capton finaly convinced them that we were all rite.

So tha disarmed us an taken us back to the Alberta houses. Tha stoped thare for dinner, an we got a square meal an a good drink of whisky. An tha buried the men I spoke of being killed thare. After we got threw with diner, the officer in comand of there outfit gave us back our armes an amanition, an sent some of his men with us to Fort Gibson, to keep the Indians from trying to take us in. The country was full of bushwhackers, as we called them. We camped one nite, an the next day went in to Fort Gibson an reported to Cornel Phillips, who was in comand of the fort. An he tuck us in at once, an gave us a good camping place an good houses.[46]

wore a pin on the front of their hunting shirts. Their original purpose was to keep political power in the hands of full-blood Indians, because they feared the influence of the whites over people of mixed blood. Late in the Civil War shortages of cloth forced many Confederate soldiers to give up their gray uniforms for butternut homespun. Pike, *Report*, 11; Rampp and Rampp, *Civil War*, 6–7; Joseph B. Thoburn, ed., "The Cherokee Question," *Chronicles of Oklahoma* 2:173.

[46] Colonel William Phillips had been an important officer from the time he was put in charge of a regiment composed largely of dissident

Tha were sevrel hunderd Indians an Negros an some whites thare. Phillips wanted to know if we wanted to inlist as solgers, or go on North an git out of the war. An some of the boys went on North with the first train that went up. An for one, I told him I wanted to inlist as a solger. Tha were sevrel of us inlisted an was swore in, I think on the 10 day of May 1864.

I wanted Phillips to a sign me to duty as a scout. He said I would receive 13 dollars a month as a in-listed man, an $5⁰⁰ a day as a scout. After we were sworn in we went to the comasery an drew clothing an armes an amanition. I was nothing but a boy. I was intitled to a bounty that I never got, but I was ignarnt and [did] not know.

I went to scouting as I were orderd by the chief of scouts. Bill Childress, a half-breed Creek Indian, was chief of scouts at that time. I think Phillips said I would be inroled in Company H, Indian Home Guards.

Editor's Note: One of the fragmentary accounts breaks off here. Another fragment, of three pages, numbered 5 on the front of one sheet and 6 and 7 on the front and back of another sheet, begins at the end of some engagement having to do with a scouting expedition. The first four and any fol-

---

Cherokees, which was mustered into the Union army as the Third Indian Home Guards. It was his troops who recaptured Fort Gibson early in 1863 and who later put down several Confederate counterattacks in the region. Kerby, *Kirby Smith*, 41, 122, 220–21; Rampp and Rampp, *Civil War*, 163–65. As JLC goes on to report, he enlisted in the Union army and joined Phillips's command a few days after he arrived at Fort Gibson.

lowing pages are lost. The fragment was part of a letter probably addressed to some government agency in Washington, D.C., attempting to establish a pension claim.

. . . I do not no whether tha got kilt or not. Me an a man by the name of Eaves went on to Fort Scott, reported to General Blair, who was in comand of the post. Thare I met up with a scout for that post by the name of Calvin Williams. He was on the eave of making a scout South under Blairs orders. It was a greed that I would come with him.[47] I remained thare until Williams got reddy to start. Tha were onley eleven of us that came threw to Texas with Capton Williams. We started for Texas a bout the last of March 65, but did not git to Texas until a bout the last of May owing to bad luck. We had trouble with the Comanche Indians. When we struck the settlements in Montague Co. Texas we learned that Lee had surenderd. The war was over. So Williams disbanded us to go home. Everything was in confusion, the Confederate army coming South. I could not git back to be musterd out an get a discharge. Tha were a man by the name of R. H. Bourdeaux in Gainesville at that time, a fine lawer.[48] After telling him all a bout my services, he said it would be all rite eney way. He could git my discharge papers an pay all the same. So he went to work on the case. He had some lawer in Washington. I think it was Charles and W. B. King of Washington.

[47] Colonel Charles White Blair (brevet brigadier general as of 13 February 1865) was for a time in command of the Second Kansas Cavalry. Mark M. Boatner, *Civil War Dictionary* (New York, 1959), 67.

[48] Richard H. Bourdeaux was practicing law in Gainesville as late as 1873. Jones, *Early Days*, 59.

Every thing went all rite, he said. He did not live but a short time after he taken the case. He died very sudently, an it seems as tho the case has been lost ever since his death. If he was corect in what he toald me, he R. H. Bourdeaux filed the statement in a proper way. This was in the year 1867 or 68. I put in a claim for my pay as a solger an scout, an one horse, bridle an sadle. As tha were no market value on horses at Fort Gibson, I did not no how to value him. I gave $75 for the horse, but the horse would bring $150 on the market here now. I think I am intitled to my discharge an pay, as I served in good faith, an pay as a solger an scout. As to what Col Phillips a greed to do in the start, when I inlisted at Fort Gibson, I was intitled to a bounty that I never got from some cause. Now you have a corect statement before you as to my services an the officers I was under. As to my transfer from Phillips comand to the 2 Kansas Regiment, the Rebs got our camp an all papers. The record at Gibson ought to show something a bout it. If I ever get eney thing, I need it now, as I am gitting old, not able to work mutch. Excuse my long letter. I had to make it long to give the substance of my services. I will send the proof with this statement. This is facts of the case.

J. L. Clark

PS   I want to state that I drew clothing the next day after I was sworn in the service at the comisary. All so armes an amanition. But I think a man by the name of Peck was acting as Quartermaster then. But I remember Mr A. W. Robb all so.

But when I got home in Texas I found some of

the oald rebbles still on the war path. Tha tride to run the yanks out, as tha called us. But we stayed with them until tha got cool. Tha was not but a fiew big fooles a mong them eney way. But I had a ruff time for 4 or 5 years to hold the fort.

2.

Editor's Note: *Although the controversy over the Great Hanging gradually subsided after the Civil War, it continued to flare up from time to time for many years. In 1916 the matter came up in the U.S. House of Representatives under circumstances that had little to do with the tragedy itself. In 1915, Congress had passed an immigration control bill that included a much-debated literacy test, but President Woodrow Wilson vetoed it. For a long while congressional conservatives attempted to muster enough support to override the veto but failed to do so. The issue was still hotly contested on the floor of the House in early 1916. Congressman John H. Stephens of the Thirteenth District of Texas, which included the Gainesville region, had entered in the* Congressional Record *a statement strongly supporting the literacy provision, in which he made anti-Catholic remarks. Representative James A. Gallivan of Massachusetts, an outspoken opponent of the literacy clause, retaliated by attacking not only Stephens but also his district as a stronghold of southern bigotry. The Great Hanging, which Gallivan knew about from a copy of Thomas Barrett's book in the Library of Congress, provided Gallivan with a perfect weapon. After delivering a long denunciation, he went so far as to intro-*

duce a bill calling for an appropriation to build a monument in Gainesville to the martyred men. For information with which to counter Gallivan's attack, Stephens made contact with J. Z. Keel, mayor of Gainesville, and others acquainted with what had happened and produced a long if lame defense of the mob's actions. The monument bill did not pass, and Gallivan probably did not expect it to, since most congressmen would have had little desire to open old wounds. But Gallivan achieved what was no doubt his prime purpose: the embarrassment of a political enemy.[1] News of the congressional controversy was published in the Gainesville Signal—*copies of which have not been located—along with commentary by a Mr. Levert, editor of the newspaper. When he read the reports in the* Signal, *James Lemuel wrote on 10 April 1916, the earliest date of writing found in his papers, a letter addressed to the "Honerble Congress" but never mailed, declaring that the men executed "was murdered by a mob of the blackest kind." The controversy led James Lemuel to write an account, dated 12 May 1916, of all he could remember or gather about the Gainesville Hanging. This account repeats and amplifies much of what he says in the letter. An edited version combining the account and the letter follows.*

May the 12, 1916

After some concideration I will rite a brief statement an give the facts in regard to the 44 good men that was murderd by a mob in Gainesville, Cooke County,

---

[1]*Congressional Record,* 53:5026–28, 5272; Appendix, 632–35, 1016–19; Gunter Papers, 222.

Texas in October 1862, as I no more a bout the men then eney body else now in this country. Will say tha were murderd for there Union princeables.

I have been asked if tha were trancient men or not. I will say tha were not. Some of them were the first settlers in Cooke Co. Tha came here from diferant states. Now it will be rememberd that in the year 1861 tha were an election to see whether Texas would go out of the Union or not. An some favord going out while the majority of the voters was in favor of the Union. An tha were speakers on boath sides of the question. I will give the names of some of them, as I remember them very well. On the Union side, tha were John C. McGee an Abe McNiece and Joe Dixon. Tha were others all so.

Now on the other side tha were Newt Chance an Greene Diamond an Jim Bourland an others. Now the Union men claimed tha got the majority, so Greene Diamond claimed to be a deligate on the rebble side, an whiped out to Austin, Texas an helped to put the state out of the Union.[2] An that caused some bad feeling on the side of the Union men. An Chance an McNiece had some pursonal trouble before that. [Chance] all so had a grudge against some of the other men that were hung in Gainesville.

Now in the sumer of 62 one O. B. Atkinson, that lived in this settlement an was a kind of a leader with

[2] JLC has the wrong first name here. James J. Diamond, not his brother Greene, was a Cooke County delegate to the Secession Convention in Austin. Another brother, W. W., was a delegate from Grayson County. Diamond, "Account," 337 n. 1, 351 n. 15.

the people here on a count of being an oald settler in this part of the country—he Atkinson organized what was called a Union League. An all Union men joined it an inrold there names, thinking it would show that tha were Union men in case the northern armey did invade Texas, an it would protect there famleys. It was threw fear of the northern armey that caused them to organise. When tha did, it was no secret. Eney man could inrole that would take the oath. Now here is what a man that inrold had to sware— so I have been toald by men that belong[ed] to the League. Swore tha were American borned, that tha never had been ingaged in eney rebellion or inserection againce the Union an Constitution of the United States of America, that tha cast there vote for the Union an Constitution of the United States of America in the year 1861.

Now that is the substance as near as I can quote it. A man by the name of Jim McPherson toald me all a bout the hole thing, as he was here all the time, was raised in this county, an was well an favorbly nown. Doutless some of the oald settlers knew him all his growing up. He belonged to the Union League himself.

His statement is this:

I was in Cooke Co, Texas a bout the 15 day of October, 1862, an was sumonds to come to Gainesville at once. I did not no for what purpose, but I went. On gitting thare I found big excitement prevailed. An after some inquiry I learned that some of my neighbors was under gard, that a man by the name of Newt Chance had got in to a grait secret. I did not no what it was, tho I knew Chance very well. Chance an Jim Bourland an some others that lived on the river were thare in town. Tha let on to be very mutch excited. You could see little groops of men talking all over town.

A long in the evning tha began to make up a jury, an tha put me an others on the jury. We had to stay all nite in town. The next day tha got all the jury. I remember some of them, as I had been aquainted with [some of them] a good while. Here is a list, as I remember: Newt Chance was made forman; Dr Thomas Barrett; a man by the name of Jones—he lived on Clear Creek; an Bill Howeth, in the timber; Reese Jones, timber. All so those men seamed to be the leaders in the matter then on hand.

I forgit the first men tha brought in for trial.[3] Newt Chance was called for a witness, and then came his statement as to how he Chance had joined the League an found out what those men was going to do. He did not speak of any Kansas men being in this part of the country at that time. But when he Chance toald his tale tha were a general confusion. I did not beleave his statement, as I had knew sevrel of the men for a long time before that. Bourland orderd me under arest. A bout that time Dr Barrett expressed his opinion an said he would not have eneything to do in the matter. So he went off an said he would not serve as a juror. But he came back in the evning an stade with them until the big slaughter came off on Sunday morning, on or a bout October 18, when tha tuck all the men tha had under gard an murderd them. In all tha were 18 with out eney trial what ever. That wound up the mob.

[3]The first men brought to trial were Dr. Henry Childs and his brother, Ephraim. Diamond, "Account," 373.

Those last men were the men that Mr Bell an the editor of the Signal had refernce to as the 20 men tha said was hung with out eney trial.

Now as to McPhersons statement. He said after some parlement a mong them selves, tha released him from under gard an made him help in the murder of a bout 18 or 20 men he McPherson saw hung. Tha confesed to being Union men til the last.

Now I intend an will have printed statements from other men an women that was rite here all the time this murder was going on. I have talked to a grait meney peple. Tha all say those men had no showing what ever. It has all ways been a mistry to me why those men that did this murdering was not brung to trial for the crime tha was gilty of. But I see the cause since I have seen Mr Keels tellagram to Mr John H. Stephens. It read like this: those 40 men were not hung for refuising to submit to the conscrip law. Now comes Mr. Levert with his note as he calles it. He sayes in big English words those forty men re-ferd to by a Massachusetts gentle man was not exe-cuted because tha refuised to cooprate with the South-ern Confederacy. But tha were an orginized gang who came here a fiew dayes previous from Kansas and had sined an oath to kill every man, woman an child on a certain nite who did not become identifide with the Union cause. He the editor sayes twenty of the men was gave a fair trial by a jury an were sentenced to hang and did hang. The citizens new that the other 20 men were as guilty as those that were found guilty, an tha were hanged with out trial. He futher sayes thare were fifty three men arested, charged with be-

[98]

ing in the plot. Before the hanging of the men, [they] acknolledged the crime an toald the whole story.

Now I will give you my note in reply to the editors note. I will ask the editor first who administerd the oath he speaks of. He seames to no so much a bout it. I say tha were not eney Kansas men in this part of the country at that time, an will ask him to prove what he published. I futher say that I have caused the record of the cort of the year 1862 to be brung out of the vault in Gainesville, an therby examined for some thing purtaining to the murder of those men. An tha is not a word on record concerning the trial in eney way.[4] Now, Mr Editor, I will ask you to show the record to sustain what you published in your note. You futher say those men acknolledged the crime an owend up. Now what did tha acknolledge? You caint mislead. You would have peple beleave tha owend up to what you acused them of in your note. Now in regard to the facts in your slang you threw out, I will say in conclusion that owing to the record an all the infermation I can gather, an what I no to be facts in the case, I will say thare is not a word of truth in your note. An I will chalenge Mr Keel an see if he has eney record to sustain his tellagram that he sent to Mr Stephens purtaining to this murder in question.

Now Keel an Levert had some object in view. I think I no what it is, but it will crop out later on. The hole thing had a handle. Why did Mr Keel an Levert jump in to this thing so red eyed. Tha knew but little a bout it. Tha either did it to slander those ded men an

[4]Since the "citizens' court" who tried the men was not constituted according to law, the records kept could not be officially recorded.

there famleys or git it down in there history. But I am here to say that it will take more than Keels tellagram an the editors note on Stephens heresay talk to put as base a lie as that in history on forty ded men.

Now we will go back to October 62. It will be re-memberd that a bout the 20 day of that month, Cornel Bill Young was shot an killed by a man by the name of Welch on Red River in this county. Welch claimed that Young an Bourland were riding on horse back threw the brakes of Hickory Creek in a trot to geather. He said he shot at Jim Bourland an hit Cornel Young.[5] Which was very unfortunate for the men tha had under gard then in Gainesville. Young· was killed on Saturday evning, an Sunday morning tha taken the men out an hung 18 at one time. Every body thought that Young would have stoped the hole thing had he not been killed. Because he turned 2 or 3 loose in the morning before he left town to go home. Cornel Young was regarded a very good man. I recolect him very well. I knew Bourland all so, went out in the state service under Cornel Bourland in 1863. I have all ways thought that Bourland was mis-led by lies that was toald on these men. The hole thing started with a lie, an some of our townsmen are seek-ing to end it the same way. I will refer you to a letter to the XLI Club in Gainesvile, dated January the 27,

[5] Welch left Cooke County just after the shooting of Colonel Young, but he was captured in east Texas and brought back to face his accusers. According to another account, Welch never confessed to the shooting. A group led by James Young, Colonel Young's son, nevertheless hanged him at the scene of the crime. It was also never established that the Union League had anything to do with the murder. The date given by JLC, 20 October, is in error; it was 16 October. Jones, *Early Days*, 65–66; Barrett, *Hanging*, 18–19; Gunter Papers, 229.

1915. I will with hold his name at this present time. He said in his letter thare was not the harmony existing between the peple on the river an the peple in the timberd sections. He said it was some thing like the feeling now existing betwen labor an capital. Doutless you will find his letter recorded with the XLI Club in Gainesville. An the man that rote the letter is a nice man, an he nos all a bout this afare.[6]

Now the editor of the Signal sayes the citisons had a hand in this black deed. I am here to say thare is not a word of truth in that statement. An he the editor caint prove that, either, because I knew very near all the peple in Gainesville an in the country at the time. Tha were as good peple in Gainesville as ever lived eney place in the world. Why not tell the truth a bout those 44 men. The whole truth is this. Tha got those oald men under gard with out eney trouble, an tha were lies toald on them threw spite an hatred that existed between Chance an Abe McNiece. I could say a grait deal more, but as the oald settlers no all a bout the facts, it is not nesasery now.

Now why doant the editor an Mr Keel use General Bill Hudsons name in some of there slang tha are throwing out to the publick? He was Brigadier General an was here in Gainesville at that time in comand over Bourland an Youngs regiments an the malisha.[7]

[6] No records of the now-defunct XLI Club have been found. During its existence in the first half of the twentieth century this club recorded and preserved many valuable items of local history.

[7] William Hudson was a Cooke County resident appointed brigadier general in 1861 and placed in command over state troops in a district whose headquarters was at Gainesville. According to Diamond, he oversaw the infiltration of the Union League and declared martial law in the area when fears of serious trouble grew. While JLC is the only source to

I can tell you why. General Hudson an Bourland an others had a big split up rite in the start. Because he Hudson was a good man, an he did not agree with there corse, an toald them so. But he was perfectly powerless an could not do eney thing with the Bour-land gang. Tha were very fiew men concerned in the mob. I can give the names of all the men concerned. Tha were no more than 6 or 8 that lived in Gaines-ville. I knew them all very well. Alec Boutwell dun the rope tying on every one that was hung before Cornel Young was shot. As to Boutwell he was runing the first saloon that ever was run in Gainesville. [He] con-tinued the buisness as long as I knew him.[8]

Editor's Note: The writer does not go on here, or anywhere else in the different accounts, to give all the names of the mob leaders.[9] He asserts in other fragments that the "mob" was "drunken" and "infuriated." In the present account he di-gresses at this point to a few details on how the hanging was carried out—details repeated in another, more extensive de-scription given below—and then turns to what he sees as the reasoning behind the mob's actions.

Now I will give my opinion a bout the hole matter. I

---

mention any objection by Hudson to the mob action in Cooke County, the general may have been responsible for the better handling of the situation in Wise County, where many were arrested but only five hanged. Elliott, "Union Sentiment," 455; Diamond, "Account," 349 n. 11, 351–52. Ac-cording to another account, General Hudson was not in Gainesville at the time. Trexler, "Episode," 249 n. 41.

[8] Alexander Boutwell had come to Texas to join the Peters Colony, becoming one of the earliest residents of what was to be Cooke County, where in 1848 he was elected the first county sheriff. Diamond, "Ac-count," 381; Smith, *First 100 Years*, 8, 14.

[9] The names of the instigators and the jurors are found in Dia-mond's account.

beleave this man McNutt that is spoken of else where in this note is the man that started the trouble. I will give my reason for it. He McNutt called a meeting for the purpose of sining the petison he had drawn up to send to the Confederate Congress. An tha met at Clem Woodses. He lived a short distance North East of Gainesville. Doutless some of the oald settlers knew him. An Mr Chance joined the League rite thare, an claimed to git posesion of there intensions. Now every body that knew Woods knew that he was a good man. Now I believe he Chance got the rong impresion as to what those mens intensions were. For I knew him when I was a boy before the war. I never herd eney body speak hard of him before this trouble come up. [The] men that met at Woodses house put there names on the petison, an rite at once the trouble begun.

Now this was not the oanly state that was dissadysfide with the exzemtion act. The peple kicked in other states. One of my neighbors, Austin Loving, sayes that law come very near to causing trouble in Mississippi, where he was at that time. But the Congress removed the law on short notice. Now it will be rememberd that some of those men that were concerned in the murder of those 44 men were big slave hoalders. An that is why I think the way I do. I think tha wanted to cary out the law. An when tha found out that the law was repealed an dun away with, tha went to work an destroyd the record, to geather with all papers purtaining to the murder. An that is why the books doant show one word purtaining to the crime.

Now it will be rememberd that when tha sent for

those men to come in, the most of them went in to see what tha wantd. When tha got to Gainesville tha found Rebs company had been orderd thare, an tha were put under gard.[10] An those that did not report was sent for an put under gard. An some of them was shot while under gard an killed. An strange to say, tha were all men that had sined this petison. Thare is a nother cause for so meney men to be killed rite in this amediate neighborhood. An that is this. The most of them were oald settlers in this county, an had fought the Indians from there door steps. An tha did not want to be crouded back on the back seat by a fiew new comers that was trying to take the lead an run the country.

Now it mite be asked by some how I knew so mutch a bout this matter. I will tell you why. My mother an foalks was rite there, an she was a cloast observer an kep a note of all things purtaining to the crime.[11]

Now as to Dr Thomas Barretts book or brief history, I have it before me an will quote the starting out part. He begins like this: "The trial an conviction an execution of forty four men in Gainesville, Texas in October 1862." He futher sayes that those men had joined a clan of Kansas Jayhawkers.[12] Tha had come

---

[10] Apparently JLC is referring to a unit or units from the rebel army. For a list of the military units that came to Gainesville at the time, see Diamond, "Account," 363–64.

[11] This account has apparently not survived.

[12] The term "jayhawker" was applied to Unionist irregulars who killed and looted on raids into southern territory. The Confederates who did likewise against the North were generally known as "bushwhackers." If the prize seemed worth it, such guerrillas were often indifferent to political sympathies, operating as no more than bandits. Military com-

here a fiew dayes previous to the time of the murder. He futher sayes that those Jayhawkers had come all the way from Kansas, an was here, an those 44 men had joined them for the purpose of murdering women an children, an had set a certain nite to do this black crime. He futher sayes tha got every thing reddy to start out on there mission, an tha come up a rain an stoped the hole thing. An tha did not go eney futher with the murdering of the women an children.[13]

Now that is what his history sayes in plain wordes. Now who can think that a fiew or a big bunch of men would come all the way from Kansas to Cooke County, Texas to do a crime like that, an let a rain, as he sayes, stop every thing? Tha must have had a dry place to stay. Stop an think how fulish it sounds to eney inteligent man. The editor of the Signal sayes in his inteligent note he published that those Kansas Jayhawkers came all the way from Kansas to do this crime, an Dr Barrett sayes tha come up a rain, an that stoped the hole thing.

Now Barrett might of had reference to Quantrill an his men. Tha came to Sherman, Texas in the summer of 62, an stade thare the most of the sumer.[14] Tha

---

manders on both sides sometimes publicly deplored the existence of these outlaws, but they made use of them when possible and often rewarded them with commissions as military officers. Kerby, *Kirby Smith*, 44–50.

[13] Barrett, *Hanging*, 10–12.

[14] William Clarke Quantrill and his band of guerrillas were seldom motivated by southern patriotism but rather by a lust for plunder and, in Quantrill's case at least, by the pleasure of killing. His activities brought him first a captain's commission in the Confederate army and then, through a visit to Jefferson Davis, a promotion to colonel. He was eventually run out of his favorite stamping ground in north Texas and was

were the oanly Kansas men that was here, an we all no how tha stood. I no tha were here in this country because tha come from here to us in the fall of 62, while Shelby was in camp at Cross Hollows in Arkansas, an stade sevrel dayes. I had a uncle that was with Quantrill all the way threw. His name was John Hicklin. He said he was very sory tha left so soon. He said if tha had a been here, tha would a stoped this Bourland mob in short order.

Editor's Note: After some repetition in almost the same words of points previously made, James Lemuel sums up his view of Barrett's account, Keel's telegram, and the newspaper editor's note.

So the publick [can] form there own opinion an call it what tha pleas. I have a name for all tha have said an dun. It looks like the boys wanted to look smart, from the stock tha tuck in the matter. I have been informed that Mr John H. Stephens read Keels tellagram aloud in the haules of Congress an made it ring like a 75 cent bell. Tha was rather surprised when tha found that Texas was a rebelious state. But tha caint dout it now.

This hole thing reminds me of a little sercumstance that hapend while I was a scout for Shelby. Tha was a man in our company. He made a good solger until we elected him first sargent in our Co. I forget his name, but we will call him Zena for short. An Zena

killed by Union guerrillas in Missouri in May 1865, while perhaps on his way to Washington to attempt the assassination of President Abraham Lincoln. Albert Castel, *William Clarke Quantrill: His Life and Times* (New York, 1962); Pete A. Y. Gunter, "The Red River Notes of Lillian Gunter" (Denton, Texas, 1977), 8.

was all ways on the look out. He thought he ought to be consulted a bout every thing, being as he was an officer. So one day Capton Bledsoe taken the battery out to drill the boys. So Zena herd them shooting blank caterages, an he tore out to see a bout it, as tha had not said eney thing to him a bout it. So he got thare an began to frisk a bout on the drill ground. Finaly he got in front of a 12 pound canon just as tha tuched it off. An it burnt the hole seat of his pants out, shirt an all. So you can gess how he looked. So he resined his office an quit the company.

But he had a dog he called Shep. An after Zena left, Shep kept barking an disturbing the camp. So finaly General Shelby gave him to the gipseys.

Editor's Note: As evidence to support his declarations concerning the hanging, James Lemuel collected eyewitness accounts from several people: Aunt Lettie Diston, Henry Jones, Parson W. C. West, and two former slaves, Frank Foreman and Bob Scott. The West account that follows combines two statements taken at different times.

Here is what Parson W. C. West said a bout the mob. He said,

I was sent for to come to Gainesville at once, a bout the first of October 1862. I went. I did not no what tha wanted, as the sumones did not say, but I went. When I got thare every thing was in confusion. I found sevrel of my neighbors thare under gard. Tha would send for them to come to town, an when tha got thare tha had a house to put them in, [on the] publick square, called the Downer Building. Tha would put them in, an had a gard a round it. I talked to some of them. Tha did not no what Bourland an Newt

Chance had them charged with, but I knew tha was all Union men an voted the Union ticket. An all so put thare names to the petison asking the Confederate Congress to remove that exzemtion law. Tha thought it unjust. I put my name to it myself. I doant no whether tha had all sined it or not, but Reese Jones was thare [in Gainesville]. He being my brother in law got me turned loose. I did not stay a bout to see what was going on.

Editor's Note: Statements from the other informants, as James Lemuel presents them, are fragmentary and digressive. I have pieced them together in a logical order.

Tha would take 4 or 5 on the wagon at a time, haul them down on a little creek in the east part of town an murder them, [then haul them back] an throw thare bodys in an oald house that was up near the square. Others would take more an hang them an haul back an forth. One of the drivers . . . was a negro. His name was Bob Scott an [he] belong to the honerable Rufus Scott. He would go to the gard house an git 2 men, haul them down to the creek . . . an take 2 dead men back an put them in the house. Tha detailed some negroes to . . . make boxes to put the first men in. Tha is one of the colord men living in Gainesville at this time, by the name of Frank Foreman, who belong to W. W. Foreman. He sayes tha made him an one other felow tare down an oald house that was in the north part of town to git lumber to make boxes. But he sayes the lumber gave out. Those men that had famleys would go an haul them out an take care of there bodys. An those that was not caried away, tha would dig a hole in the bank of the creek, an rap them in a blanket an throw a little dirt on them an go on with there bloody work. Tha made [Foreman] help dig holes in the creek bank. An Mrs Diston sayes the hogs was

[108]

seen with her step fathers arm draging it over town after he was buried.

[After Welch shot Colonel Young,] Jim Youngs Company came in from the Territory an taken 19 men that Bourland had under gard an shot an hung every one of them at one time.

Now this is the facts, be cause my mothers history tells the same thing.

I will conclude by giving the names of all the men that I pursnoly knew an others that was murdered . . . . In the beginning [I] will give the names of the first settlers that lived in this county when my father came:

One of our near neighbors was William Rhodes. He [came] from North Carolina here, an got 320 acres of land as a home stead from the state. He had a nice famley an his oaldest boy belong to the same company that I belonged to. Now Rhodes sold land to a man by the name of Eli Scott a bout the time the war started. An Scott moved to the land an was murderd while he lived on the land. He Scott [came] from California here, an had a big famley, an was nice foalks. Him an Rhodes were hung the same day. Tha are boath buried on the Rhodes survey, now owned by Sam McClerran.

The next neighbor I will name was Hiram Kilborn. He had a home stead of 320 acres of land patened to him by the state. Tho tha did not hang him. He was shot an killed by some of the Bourland men in trying to git a way. His foalks never got his body an did not no what tha dun with it. He Kilborn was a

Babtist preacher, and not one of the kind that preached for the money that was in it. He was the oanly Babtist preacher in this country when we came here. I am informed by Frank Foreman that [he] helped to bury Kilborn.

I will give the names [of others who were hanged] as follows:

Wernell—160 acres
Richard Martin—landholder
Oald Grandpaw Burch—would talk, say what he thought—landholder
H. J. Esmond—320 acres
Ward
Evans—Or Quinn
Clem Woods—landholder
Wolsey—landholder
Manon—lived on Preston Road
Oald man Leffel
A. B. McNiece—landholder
Wash Morris—landholder
Wesley Morris—landholder—tha were brothers
Thomas Floyd—shot while under gard—landholder
John Crisp—landholder
James Powers
Rama Dye—oald man—landholder
J. Dawson
Oald Man Wiley—landholder
J. Morris
Barnes
Milburn

W. Anderson

Gross

Ward

Dr. Johnson—nation [probably from the "Indian Nation"]

Childs, Senior

Childs, Junior

Hampton

Locke

Foster

Fields

D. Anderson

D. Taylor

R. Manton

Jones

Carmichael

Henry Cochran

Those names are as tha was gave to me by Mc-Pherson.

Will McCool an two others were murderd at Bill Young Spring on the river after Welch killed Young in Bourland Hollow. [I] doant no a bout there land.[15]

Editor's Note: To end the letter to Congress from which one list of the names of the hanged is taken, James Lemuel, after reporting the above names, goes on to conclude as follows.

[15] JLC often mentions a total of forty-four. This list is not complete and may contain some errors in names. Even the number of men murdered is not known exactly. The best authorities here seem to be Barrett, *Hanging*, 21, and Wheeler's diary entry for 19 October 1862. Both accounts give forty as the number hanged and add that two were shot while trying to escape. If two were hanged by the military, the numbers then agree. According to Diamond, three men were hanged by the military. Diamond, "Account," 402.

Now to give some idea as to how things was caried on at the time of the linchen, Oald Man W. W. Wernel, whoes name is on the list, was hung in Gainesville an braught to his wife an children. The men that brung him went an buried him, an put his head north. Tha said he wanted to go north an tha would put his head north. His grave is here to show the facts. . . .

You will please excuse bad spelling an writing to geather with my boaldness in writing this letter. Eney thing I can do please command me.

J. L. Clark

Editor's Note: *Three letters from James Lemuel to his family touching on the hanging have survived, written from Arkansas while he was serving there in the Confederate army between November 1862 and March 1863. Beginning on the last sheet of the second of these letters, his mother began a letter of her own to her dead husband's brothers and sisters, who lived in another but unidentified part of Texas. The continuation of her letter past the first page has been lost.*

Dardanelle Arkansas

Sunday November the 23rd 1862
Dear Father and Mother

It is with the greatest of pleasure I write to you this morning. I am not verry well at present. I have had the measels but am getting well again. I am able to get up and walk about. And with the propper care taken of myself I think I will be well in a few days. I hope this will find you well. I am at Dardanelle, Arkansas a little town on the Arkansas river. The citisens of this town have been as kind to me as people could be. Pe Rodes has the measels. With this exception the Cooke County Boys are all well.

I would like to be at home verry well, but I dont expect I will be at home untill peace is made. I have heard that there had been several men hung in Cooke County. Write to me and tell me all that are hung that I am acquainted with. And when you write direct your letters to Dardanelle, Yell County, Arkansas. Just back it like any other letter. Dont put the regiment or company on it for if you do it will have to go to the regiment and might not come here at all.

Our company has been ordered here from the regiment, for what purpose we do not know, unless it is to catch deserters. It is said that the mountains are full of them about here. There is no company here but ours. . . . [I] like to stay here better than any place I have seen since I left home and I believe this is a general thing with all the boys. And I think we will stay here all this winter. There has already been some scouting parties sent out since we have been here.

I have not much of Importance to write but I want you to write to me as soon as you posabley can, given me all the news you can think of.

You must excuse my short letter and I will try to write more the next time.

Give my best respects to all enquiring friends and tell Pe Rodeses folks he sends his best love and respects to them. So no more at present but still remains your affectionate Son untill death.

James L. Clark to N. M.
Clark and family

Dardanelle Arkansas   January the 2nd 1863

Dear Mother brothers and
sisters

I have just received your kind letter of December the 12th. I was glad to hear from you and that you was well, but oh the horrors and agonies of my heart at hearing of the cruel murder of my Father no tongue can tell. Mother what to do. I am at a loss. Your condition is dreadfull but thank heaven there is a just god to whome the blood of my dear Father and tears of a deeply injured family cry for vengence. Men who have no more feelings of humanity than they have deserve to be cast into the very depths of the gulf of perdition. It seems as if it is out of my power to come home at present but I will come home as soon as I posabley can. Mother God bless you and keep you by his tender care. I dont know how you are going to get along but do the best you can and when I get home you shall not suffer if it is in my power to keep you from suffering.

It does seem hard. It seems cruel that we are treated so. While I am here battleing in defence of my country those cruel fiends, those tools of hell should dare to murder, yes to dip there hands in the blood of our best citizens. My Father was no northern man. He was for peace and did not believe in brother killing brother or the Father the son. But what am I saying. My words amount to nothing. Yes those deeds will long be remembered. Our troops here are deserting every hour yet not a man of [our] Company have deserted yet and will not desert. Now you see who are the traitors to their country. Our company has been

[114]

branded with the name of traitors to their country by the hellhounds of Gainesville. They are of no use to their country. They are fitten for nothing but to do those deeds which are too mean for a negro to be allowed to do.

Mother I will come home as soon as posable but will not desert my country.

Give my best respects to all enquireing friends and reserve a double portion for yourself. I remain your affectionate son untill death.

James L Clark to C[ordelia]
Hulda Clark and family

P.S. I have clothes plenty for the present and if I had not I could not get them from home.

Editor's Note: *The fragment of the letter from James Lemuel's mother follows*:

Cook County Texas   Feb the 17   1863

Dear brother and sisters, I take the opportunity of dropping you a fiew lines to let you now that we are well at this time, hopping these fiew lines may find you enjoying the same blessing. I have no news to write. Times is hard. I hird that some of the men at Gainesville was a going to administer on the mens property that was hung. If thay do I want you to come and tend to it for me. I dont want them gentlemen to have any thing that I have got[16] I want you to come if you can. Tell Evaline and Cynthia if they knowed how

---

[16] Both the Union and the Confederacy passed laws permitting confiscation of the property of those convicted of treason against the government. Apparently no serious attempt was ever made to confiscate the property of the victims of the Great Hanging.

lonesome I was they would come and stay with me. I want them to be shure and come. Elviry I want you to come to. And hury up Lem and come on. The children is lonesome and dissatisfied and wants to see you verry bad. I thought I would send Lemuel letter so you could read it and when you comes bring it back. I dont now whare he is to write to you. But when I hear I will write to you. Thay had to leave Dardanelle. I want you to bring me a hundred pounds of shorts if they are any cheaper down thare. Thay are 4 dollars a hundred up here and cant get much of them at that. Cotton is from a shilling to. . . .[17]

Camp Porter March the 20th [18] 63
near Batesville [Arkansas]

Dearest Mother Sisters and Brothers

It is with much pleasure that I seat myself to drop you a few lines, to let you know how I am getting along. This leaves me well at present. Fondly hoping they may [find] you all enjoying the same blessings and doing well. We are still in camps near Batesville but it is thought by a great many that we will start to Missouri pretty soon. We are drilling six hours a day, Infantry drill, and it goes pretty hard with us. Captain

[17]Shorts was a type of bran used as animal food. Before the American Revolution the most prevalent money in the Colonies was not English but the Spanish dollar and its fractional coins. Still people reckoned in so many "shillings" to a dollar, the number varying from colony to colony, and this practice went on for a long time after independence. The true division of the Spanish dollar was into eight reales worth twelve and one-half cents each. This same fraction of the American dollar came to be called a "bit" by many, but in some parts of the South, following long custom, it continued to be known as a "shilling," which is probably the usage intended here.

McMahan has just come in from Mo and he saw a late St Louis Democrat and it stated that Lincoln had made a proposal to our President for an Armistice. It also said he would acceed to it if Lincoln would remove all federal troops from off Southern soil. It states that all hopes of taking Vicksburg had been abandoned by the Federals.

Mother tell George Kilborns folks that he is still with us but it not verry well. He has a verry bad cough and it is thought by some that he has Consumption. But he is able to go about. He has not been able to do any duty since he left Home but has been able to stay with us. Mother I would like to see you all verry much and I hope it wont be long before I can come home to stay. And if ever I do ever get Home again I think I will be satisfied to stay. You must write to me soon and Direct your letters to Little Rock, Capt J. T. Crisps Co, Thompsons Reg, Shelby Brigade.

Tell Georges Father and Mother to write him, for he wants to hear from them verry bad. He has not heard from them since he left Home. And be sure to Direct your letters by way of Little Rock or they wont get here. Give our best respects to all of our friends and our best respects to you all. So no more at present but remains your son till Death   J. L. Clark

Editor's Note: George A. Kilborn appended the following note to James Lemuel's letter:

Be sure and tell my Father and Mother to write to me as soon as you get this letter and tell them where I am. I send my best respects to you and your family.

Geo. A. Kilborn

Index